"*Success Strategies for College and Beyond* contains down-to-earth, practical, easy-to-understand, and quick-to-implement steps to success. Joan Gustafson writes from experience, giving you the keys to success in simple language that will enable you to start implementing these strategies today."
　　—Jill Lublin
　　Best-selling author, *Guerrilla Publicity* and *Networking Magic*
　　Host, *Do the Dream* radio show and *GoodNews TV*

"Wow! What a profound book! There is no doubt in my mind that when the readers apply the principles contained in the book, they will absolutely achieve success in their endeavors. More importantly, they will successfully create a peaceful, harmonious, enthusiastic life filled with wonderful experiences."
　　– Dean R. Portinga, Th.D., Ph.D.

"What a great advantage for college students to have a book like this to help them on their life's journey. *Success Strategies for College and Beyond* contains information that is absolutely critical to success in every aspect of life. I highly recommend it to students or anyone."
　　—Bobbie R. Stevens, Ph.D.
　　President, Unlimited Futures LLC
　　Author, *Unlimited Futures: How to Understand the Life You Have and Create the Life You Want*

"If you're just entering 'the real world,' Joan Gustafson provides 'real success stories' and 'real simple steps' to make it and make it big, no matter what your aspirations are. When Joan interviewed me for this book, she pulled everything out of me to share with you, and I know she did this with the other twenty-seven people she interviewed. I just wish I had a book like this to help me when I graduated from college."
—Michael Norwood, D.C.
Author, *The Wealthy Soul* series

"This book is an invaluable tool for the person who believes they can succeed and is open to pursue their goals. The organization and ideas are true steps to success. Joan Gustafson has challenged her readers to achieve the possibilities. I wish this book was available when I was making decisions that changed my life; I really believe that success would not have taken me so long."
—Annie O'Connor, PT, OCS
Corporate director, Musculoskeletal Practice Rehabilitation Institute of Chicago

"I just could not put this book down! As I was reading it, I was getting so many ideas that I couldn't decide if I should read on or stop myself and totally digest what I had read. College students are fortunate to have this book at this point in their lives."
—Marilyn Straka
Founder and president, On The Level

What readers are saying about
Success Strategies for College and Beyond

"This is a book that every college student in America needs to read. Joan Gustafson will lead you on a path to create a successful future and live your dreams! Read this book, and then read it again!"
—James Malinchak
Author, *From College to the Real World*
Contributing editor, *Chicken Soup for the College Soul*
Past two-time College Speaker of the Year winner
(*Campus Activities* magazine and the APCA)

"Joan Gustafson has masterfully created an interesting, stimulating, and powerful guide—a set of 'best practices' for students who want to experience success in college and throughout their lives. A must for every student's backpack!"
—K. D. Taylor
Associate Dean, Utah Valley State College

"This book is fantastic! At first, I thought I would skim through it, but I couldn't put it down. Joan Gustafson has done a fantastic job of bringing together insights from many sources and many streams of literature to provide the reader with great value on every page. The book is a breath of fresh air in our hurried lives, a chance to sit and think about what matters and how to make what matters a part of our every day, starting from Day 1 as a college freshman."
—Pamela W. Henderson, Ph.D.
Associate professor of Business, Washington State University
CEO, New Angle Inc.

"*Success Strategies for College and Beyond* drives home a lot of valuable points regarding personal development that are essential to success in life. This book is a most valuable asset to college students and, quite frankly, to a lot of well-established folks who could do better in life. This book would make a great college course, and, if up to me, I would make it mandatory for all college freshmen."
—Jim Paschal
Aircraft designer

"An extremely successful woman, Joan Gustafson comes from a deep level of understanding of what it takes to be successful, and she instills this understanding through *Success Strategies for College and Beyond*. I've learned that, if you implement these strategies, you will be successful, no matter what happens in your life."
—Michael Starkweather
Patent attorney and college professor

"*Success Strategies for College and Beyond* should be titled "If I Knew Then What I Know Now." This book is jam-packed with a plethora of useful and important information you can start using right now. Joan Gustafson has expertly relayed her experiences, as well as those of other successful people, to demonstrate what is needed to become successful. Success is not luck, but determination and having goals and a plan to attain them. If you're serious about succeeding in college and beyond, you need this book."
—Becky Creighton
Real estate investor

Success Strategies for College and Beyond

Success Strategies for College and Beyond

Joan Eleanor Gustafson

Leader Dynamics

ISBN: 0-9703026-4-9

Library of Congress Catalog Control Number: 2004098736

Cover design: OspreyDesign

Book production: Tabby House

Other books by Joan Eleanor Gustafson

- *A Woman Can Do That! 10 Strategies for Creating Success in Your Life*

- *Some Leaders Are Born Women! Stories and Strategies for Building the Leader within You*

- *Success without Struggle™: How to Control your Destiny through Your Attitude* (e-book)

- *Success Is a Decision of the Mind* (co-authored with other success specialists)

- *Taking Charge: Lessons in Leadership* (co-authored with other leadership specialists)

Leader Dynamics
Phoenix, Arizona

Dedication

To my grandson, Ethan,
a successful second-grader,
who is building the foundation
for success in college and beyond

Acknowledgments

When I decided to write my first book, I mistakenly thought it would be a lonely process as I envisioned myself sitting alone at my computer transcribing my thoughts through the use of the keyboard. I soon learned that a book is the combined effort of many people working together as a team, with each member caring passionately about the final results. This book is no exception. I am grateful to all those who have been an inspiration to me and those who have contributed to fulfilling my vision of a book that will help college students create success in their lives.

To gather examples of the application of the strategies in this book, I interviewed twenty-nine successful college students and graduates through questionnaires and/or telephone conversations. They unselfishly shared their lives and insights with me so that others may benefit. Although I did not know many of these people before the interviews, I now consider them my friends and appreciate their individual and collective contributions. A special thanks to each of them: Sara Arbel, Lois Crandell, Becky Creighton, Gayle Crowell, Dr. Jeanne Elnadry, Keith Geilman, Christina Gerrish, Mishana Hosseinioun, Nicholas Kahler, Stephanie Kane, Dan Love, Jill Lublin, Dr. Michael Norwood, Carol Notto, Jeff Notto, Annie O'Connor, Rebecca O'Neill, Jim Paschal, Dr. Dean Portinga, Wendy Franz Richards, Dr. Bobbie Stevens, Marilyn Straka, Marcy Swan, Charleen Tajiri, K. D. Taylor, Dr. Kathy Brittain White, Laurie Windham, Connie Wolf, and Dr. Nathan Wood.

Many thanks to my family, friends, and colleagues who gave of their time by transcribing interviews and proofreading early versions of the manuscript: Gloria Aguirre, Shelley Berube, Carolyn Jensen, and Cynthia Metcalf.

Finally, there aren't enough words in the English language to say how grateful I am to my husband, Cliff Gustafson, who always supports me in everything I choose to do.

Contents

Introduction   *xv*

Chapter One: Believe in Yourself!   23

Chapter Two: Dare to Dream!   41

Chapter Three: Determine Your Priorities!   63

Chapter Four: Set Powerful Goals!   79

Chapter Five: Ready—Aim—Take Action!   97

Chapter Six: Stay Focused!   113

Chapter Seven: Remain Positive, No Matter What!   123

Chapter Eight: Live Your Life with Integrity!   141

Chapter Nine: Enjoy the Moment!   153

Chapter Ten: Continue to Learn!   167

Chapter Eleven: Increase Your Success!   177

Appendices

   A: Advice to Students   181

   B: Reference Guide to Creating Success in Your Life   189

   C: Decision Analysis Chart   197

   D: Recommended Reading   199

Index   201

About the Author   213

Introduction

Success Strategies for College and Beyond

When I was in ninth grade, I made a decision on what I thought would be my lifelong career. It was in the fall of that year that I had the opportunity to go to work with my uncle Ralph one day. Uncle Ralph had been my idol since I was a small child. Thinking back to my fourth birthday, I remember the letter he sent me from his Marine Corps base. What an exciting life he seemed to live!

At the time I went to work with Ralph, he was a computer systems engineer. This was during the era of first-generation computers, when a computer filled a room the size of a gymnasium and had a minute fraction of the power of today's handheld computer. However, even without knowing that computer power would take giant leaps forward as technology accelerated over the next several years, I was impressed and intrigued with this fascinating machine.

Ralph demonstrated the "control center" for the computer, which was a console typewriter device in the middle of the room. To enhance his demonstration, he instructed me to type my name on this console. He had previously programmed the computer to give me information about my family and myself when it recognized my first name. I was amazed that the computer knew so much about me, and I understood that Ralph had been the one to teach the computer what it knew.

On the drive home, I told my uncle that I had decided that day that I also wanted to work with computers. After hearing of my decision, he hesitated for a moment before speaking. He finally decided that this was a field in which I could excel, even though very few women had pursued it before that time. However, he cautioned me that I would need to do very well in college in order to be accepted into this field.

At age fourteen, I set my goals to excel in high school and to major in mathematics in college, as there was not yet an existing course of study for the computer profession. After accomplishing my high school goal, I took a long detour to accomplishing my college goal. One of my high school graduation gifts was an engagement ring. Since I had been dating this man for five months and didn't want to hurt his feelings, I agreed to marry him. Shortly after we were married, I learned that my husband was deeply in debt, and all of his income was needed to pay his past expenses. This meant that I needed to work full time to support the two of us, and we had no money to pay for a college education. I gave up on my goal of earning a college degree.

When the marriage ended in divorce, I found myself in the role of a single mother and continued to be the breadwinner for my family. Feeling sorry for myself, I became physically ill, undergoing more than a dozen surgeries, complicated by asthma, pneumonia, chronic bronchitis, and sudden deafness in one ear. I spent much of my twenties in hospitals until my doctor diagnosed me with a serious heart condition and ordered that I quit my job.

For some time afterward, I continued to feel sorry for myself and to question why this could happen to someone who had my goals and aspirations. Although I never will know the answer to this, I finally did realize that, if I was going to ever successfully accomplish my goals, I was the one who was going to make this happen. With this realization, I began working on strategies for success.

Armed with these strategies, I began to recover and to start walking on the pathway to success. Within a few months, I had my doctor's approval to return to work, at first part time and then full time. I attended college classes at night, and earned both my bachelor's and master's degrees while I was working full-time and raising my children. In succession, I became a computer programmer, a systems analyst, and a systems supervisor. After completing my MBA degree, I transferred into marketing and moved up the corporate ladder to an international marketing management position.

I recently retired from a high-ranking management position in a large, multinational corporation. If success would be measured in financial income and material possessions alone, I would rank among the most successful American women of my generation. My annual income has been in the top 1 percent of that of all Americans throughout most of my career. I have lived and worked in Europe, as well as in the United States, and have received numerous awards for leadership. Over the past several years, I have owned two or three houses simultaneously in various parts of the United States, and my husband and I have traveled extensively around the world. In addition, I am blessed with more important, nonmaterial gifts of life—a loving husband, wonderful children, and beautiful grandchildren.

Although many people believe that success is predetermined and that successful people are born, not made, this was not true for me. My beginnings in life were humble. I have met many people, who complain that they are not able to earn a college degree because of finances. I was one of those people until I learned that there are countless alternatives for financing a college education.

I was a shy child, and I carried this shyness into adulthood. I also had low self-esteem, an extraordinarily high fear of rejection, and a strong desire to please other people. I was a perfectionist and worked hard to succeed. I excelled at my full-time job and at the university courses I took at night. Between work and school, I helped my children with their homework, maintained a relatively spotless house, and cooked well-balanced meals.

After making many mistakes throughout most of my earlier adult life, I adopted and integrated ten basic strategies for success.

The strategies did not come to me all at once, but rather through a process as I began to determine what I really wanted in life. As I began to use these strategies one-by-one, I started to enjoy more success. By integrating the strategies, I have been able to exceed all of my previous goals and dreams. I have also enjoyed observing the success of other people I have trained and coached as they have incorporated these strategies into their lives. The integrated strategies work well for students who want to be successful in college, as well as in their lives beyond college.

This book is based on my experience and research, as well as on interviews with highly successful college students and graduates. Strategies, principles, and tips for success are integrated into the text to assist you in developing a personal action plan to achieve your goals and create success in college and in your life.

The interviewees agree that success is different for each person and that each of us needs to determine our own definition of success. The following definitions are samples from my interviews with these students and graduates:

- *Success is being able to look at the person in the mirror every morning and feel good that you are achieving what you set out to achieve and done so in an honorable way.*
- *Success is a feeling of continually moving forward but the ability to be happy standing still.*
- *Success is positive contribution to self, society, and the environment.*
- *Success is feeling happy each day.*
- *Success is a feeling of accomplishment and fulfillment.*
- *Success is the achievement of goals that are important to you.*
- *Success is living comfortably with who you are and what you have.*
- *Success is not only having a fulfilling career where I know I am making a difference, but it's also having time*

- *to pursue outside interests.*
- *Success is having peace of mind, free from unnecessary concern over the future and being able to dwell in the now moment.*
- *Success is when both my work and my personal life are fulfilling.*
- *Success is a balance in personal and professional life.*
- *Success is being known as a person with values and integrity.*
- *Success is a mental, physical, emotional, and spiritual balance in one's life.*
- *Success is enjoying each day.*
- *Business success is achieving a position in a profession the individual enjoys.*
- *Success is maintaining personally acceptable levels of progress toward identifiable personal goals.*
- *If I can positively touch one person, plant a seed, or do a good act each day, then that day is successful.*
- *Success is the quiet peace of knowing I did my absolute best.*
- *Success is achieving one's full potential.*

Although these definitions of success and the integration of the strategies in the following chapters apply to everyone, this book is written primarily for college students.

My purpose in writing this book is to assist students in creating success in their lives and in taking responsibility for their own success. By using and integrating the strategies in this book, a student can achieve success, both in college and in the world.

In addition to defining a new paradigm for success, in which measurement is based on your own definition of success rather than on the perceived expectations of others, *Success Strategies for College and Beyond* will help you by doing the following:

- Giving strategies and examples on how to be successful both in college and in life.
- Assisting you to realize that success comes from within—and giving tips on how you can make this happen.

- Giving examples on how a student can achieve success, regardless of things that have happened in the past.
- Demonstrating that success is available to each of us and that it is possible to be a winner without someone else having to lose.

The students and graduates in this book come from different backgrounds and are from different colleges. They have made different choices in their lives. They have overcome different obstacles and have made different mistakes. Yet, they subscribe to similar value systems and principles, which have been major factors in their success. In the following chapters, they share these values and principles in order to assist more students to achieve success, as each of these students and graduates are now doing. During the interviews, the following students and graduates offered valuable tips and examples on the various strategies, which are described in the chapters ahead:

- Lois Crandell
- Becky Creighton
- Gayle Crowell
- Jeanne Elnadry, M.D.
- Keith Geilman
- Christina Gerrish
- Mishana Hosseinioun
- Nicholas Kahler
- Stephanie Kane
- Dan Love
- Jill Lublin
- Michael Norwood, D.C.
- Carol Notto
- Jeff Notto
- Annie O'Connor, P.T., OCS
- Rebecca O'Neill, J.D.
- Jim Paschal
- Dean Portinga, Th.D., Ph.D.
- Wendy Franz Richards
- Bobbie Stevens, Ph.D.
- Marilyn Straka
- Marcy Swan
- Charlene Tajiri
- K. D. Taylor
- Kathy Brittain White, Ph.D.
- Laurie Windham
- Connie Wolf
- Nathan Wood, Ph.D.

These college students and graduates have created success in their lives by using the strategies described in *Success Strategies for College and Beyond*. You can, too, if you are committed.

Each of the next ten chapters contains a separate strategy, along with instructions and/or suggestions on how to implement the strategy to create the success you want for yourself. As you read each chapter, you will engage in exercises or ponder some tips related to the strategy introduced in that chapter. You will also be integrating the strategy with those from previous chapters. Since each chapter builds on the strategies of previous chapters, I recommend that you read the chapters in sequence.

The strategies, as listed below, have the potential to change your life as you adopt and integrate them:

- Believe in Yourself!
- Dare to Dream!
- Determine Your Priorities!
- Set Powerful Goals!
- Ready—Aim—Take Action!
- Stay Focused!
- Remain Positive, No Matter What!
- Live Your Life with Integrity!
- Enjoy the Moment!
- Continue to Learn!

These strategies are simple, but they take some time to implement and integrate. Success is not instantaneous; rather, it is a process that requires commitment and work. The results are well worth the effort. Are you ready to create more success in college and in your life? If so, turn the page, and let's get started!

Chapter One

Believe in Yourself!

Self-confidence can be learned

At a very young age, Michael Norwood knew he was born to be a writer. He was only nine years old when he wrote his first novel, and he loved doing it. He later started writing magazine articles, and his first one was published when he was sixteen. By then, he had been writing for ten years, with his only feedback coming from teachers, who told him that his grammar was poor.

Michael had one sibling, a sister, who was diagnosed with cancer when he was ten. He spent the next six years watching his beloved sister become more ill until finally she was gone. While going through this trauma, he kept telling himself that there had to be a different way to treat this. He started looking into alternative medicine with the hope that he would be able to prevent someone else from suffering as his sister had. He decided to become a doctor of chiropractic.

An excellent student, Michael was able to skip a few years of school and start college early. When he graduated from Life Chiropractic College, Dr. Michael Norwood was the youngest chiropractor in the country. He became a very successful chiropractor, specializing in kinesiology.

Although Michael loved his career in chiropractic, he knew that the true love of his life was still his writing. After many years of practicing chiropractic, Michael decided to become a full-time writer. His *Wealthy Soul* series of books has enhanced the lives of countless people.

The dictionary defines success in terms of achievement, fame, and prosperity. Michael defines success as the feeling of continual motion forward but the ability to be happy standing still. Regardless of the definition, Michael was a successful college student and a successful chiropractor, and he is definitely a successful writer.

Laurie Windham was destined to be a star. It seemed that she was born with an amazing talent when she started singing before she could walk or talk. She was an unusually gifted child and shared her talent by singing for relatives and friends while she was still in preschool. She enhanced her skills through countless hours of practice. By the age of twelve, she was performing in professional theater. She loved music and lived music. Her ultimate enjoyment in life was the time she spent performing. Because of her remarkable talent, the University of Texas granted her a scholarship in vocal performance.

A mezzo-soprano, Laurie sang a broad range of music from classical/opera to musical comedy to rock. In college, she performed in musicals, including *Camelot*, *The Boyfriend*, and *Once upon a Mattress*. She thoroughly enjoyed what she was doing and assumed that music would always be her profession and livelihood.

As a cheerleader in school, Laurie began to strain her voice. In addition, she suffered from chronic throat infections; nonetheless, she continued to sing, causing irreparable damage to her voice and throat. While in college, she had surgery to remove an abscess and scar tissue from her throat, thus leaving her unable to sing for over a year. She then attempted to continue her college studies in voice for the next two years, at which time the vocal performance professors at the University of Texas advised her that she did not have enough voice left to fulfill her dreams and aspirations.

"As you might expect," Laurie said, "this was a devastating blow. Up to that point in my life, I—and everyone who knew me—had defined me as a performer. I had never tried very hard in school to be good at anything else. I truly saw my career as being on the stage. When that was no longer an option, it created a serious identity crisis for me."

To salvage the college credits she had earned in music, Laurie changed her major from music to music therapy, a field that uses music as a therapeutic tool with disabled people. After working as a registered music therapist for four years, she began to evaluate alternative careers and decided to learn about the business world. She was soon accepted into the MBA program at Louisiana State University. Because she had not previously considered a career in business, Laurie knew that she had a challenge ahead of her. She rose to this challenge.

When I met Laurie, she was the president of a leading marketing and management consulting company in the San Francisco area. She was working with international companies, including Cisco Systems and Oracle Corporation. In addition to consulting, she had initiated a quarterly newsletter on e-Business and had begun funding ongoing customer research in that area. Laurie has written and published two books on e-Business and is a sought-after speaker for conferences throughout the United States, Asia, and South America. Laurie is an extremely successful woman, and she has engineered that success herself.

Michael Norwood and Laurie Windham grew up in different parts of the United States. They attended different colleges for different reasons. Their backgrounds and career choices are completely different. Because of circumstances and personal choice, their careers are different from those they had originally planned when they started college. However, both are extremely successful, not only in their careers, but also in life.

Believing in oneself is the foundation strategy for success in college, in a career, and in life. The successful college students and graduates, who interviewed for this book, all have that foundation. An example is K. D. Taylor, who graduated from Brigham Young University, and now is associate dean of the School of General Academics at Utah Valley State College. K. D. said, "I know I am not the brightest, the most sophisticated, or the most capable person in any given setting, but I believe I can accomplish whatever I choose to pursue. If I really want to achieve a goal, I know I can make it happen if I give enough effort to it. I believe in my own capability to succeed. To me, it's never a question of whether I can do something, but rather, whether I want to do it enough to see it through. My belief in myself always gives me the courage to start a new goal."

K. D. demonstrated her self-confidence when she became a volunteer firefighter and EMT after the age of fifty. "I noticed, after a fire close to our home, that our small fire department needed more volunteers," she said. "I applied to the city fire department, took classes, and attended many training sessions to become qualified as a volunteer firefighter. It was physically challenging, but I felt confident that I would make a contribution. Despite the tremendously hard work, I enjoyed learning the principles and skills, and have been actively involved in fighting fires in the past few years. My involvement encouraged two other women and a husband to join. One of those women has become a training officer for the department."

Many of us think that others have more self-confidence than we do. After all, other people were born into families with more money, have doting parents, and are more popular. Others are smarter, have a higher IQ, or are better looking. Maybe their professors like them better, or they are always in the right place at the right time.

The truth is that self-confidence is available to each of us. Every one of us has the ability to become a Michael Norwood or a Laurie Windham. It doesn't matter where or when we were born. Our social background does not matter. Our financial background does not matter. It does not even matter if we have made huge mistakes in our lives. Each of us can develop the self-confidence needed to succeed in college and in life. The following tips will help you get started on this.

I. Think of yourself as the important person you are.

Many of us grow up believing that other people are more important than we are. There are many reasons for this. Some of us claim that we were conditioned to believe this way. Some of us think that we just were not given a fair chance in life. Some of us grow up with an inferiority complex that we think is impossible to overcome. Regardless of the reason, we have a hard time believing that we are as important as anyone else.

From the time I was fourteen years old, my goal was to become a computer programmer. Since this was during the early days of computers when there was no computer science curriculum, my plan was to major in mathematics in order to achieve my goal. However, at age nineteen, I married a man who was deeply in debt. At that time, I had completed one year of college. In order to survive, I had to work full time and could not afford to continue my education. I accepted a position with the state of Minnesota and spent my days documenting accident reports and studying traffic patterns.

After almost two years, I was able to resume my education by taking night classes at the University of Minnesota while I worked full time during the day. In the next three years, I took every math, statistics, and computer class that was offered. I was excited to learn that the state Civil Service Department was testing for a computer programmer position, which was to be filled within the next month. I saw this as a potential opportunity to meet my goal before I finished my college degree. I took the test and thought I had done well.

My heart was pounding as I opened the letter that contained the test results. To my dismay, the letter said that I had not received a passing score. When I shared the disappointing news with a colleague at work, he suggested that I go to the Civil Service office to review the test results. "I can't do that," I replied. "They're Civil Service, and they're always right." I was really saying that the person who scored the test knew more than I did, was more important than I was, and was not to be bothered by an unimportant person like me.

Through some major coaxing and an offer to do the talking for me, my friend enticed me to go together with him to visit the Civil Service office. There I learned that the score for this test had been based on a combination of three criteria. The written test was 50 percent of the score, related education was 40 percent, and length of state employment was 10 percent. I had scored the highest score ever on the written test! I had been given five points for my five years of state employment. However, since the Civil Service Department had no record of my having attended college, my educational score was zero. Therefore, my total score was 55 percent. A score of 70 percent was needed to pass. With this new information, I was quickly able to transfer my college transcripts from the University of Minnesota to the State Civil Service Department, raising my total score by forty points. Within one week, I was offered the computer programmer position.

The rest of my life would have been different had I not visited the Civil Service office to inquire on the reason for my test score. Because I believed that other people were more important than I was, I didn't want to disturb them to inquire about something that meant even this much to me. Through this experience, I learned some valuable lessons. One of the main ones was that I am also an important person, and I needed to recognize this myself. Knowing this has opened many doors for me and, in turn, has contributed greatly to my success.

Becky Creighton, a successful real estate investor, graduated from Ohio State University. Her college graduation stands out as her most significant accomplishment. She said, "It took five-and-one-half years, but I made it! I remember when I was a senior in high school applying to Ohio State, and I was rejected five times. I kept calling them every week asking if they would admit me. Since I was an out-of-state student, the admission standards were much higher for me than if I had been an in-state student. Finally, one week before dorm contracts were due, I received a thick envelope that contained my acceptance letter and dorm information. Once I knew I was in, I knew I would graduate."

The fear of rejection for most people is so strong that many of them never even try. If you fear rejection, remember Becky. She knew she could make it, and she did not give up until she did.

Know that you are an amazing human being and that you can accomplish whatever is important to you. Christina Gerrish, a student at the Art Institute of Phoenix, said, "By believing every day that I can do this and that I will make my future better, it pushes me to try harder and to do better in school."

K. D. Taylor reiterated, "I have a positive sense of capability to succeed. The question has never been whether I could succeed, but rather, whether I chose to do what was required to succeed. I have always felt I could accomplish whatever I really wanted to, if I felt strongly enough about it, and if I was willing to put forth the effort needed."

Marcy Swan's favorite motto is, "I am only one, but I AM one." She genuinely believes she can make a difference, first by deciding which activity to pursue, and then by taking the steps necessary to make it happen. Marcy, a graduate of Brigham Young University, adds value in the world by training foster parents and providing shelter care.

After receiving inner direction that she needed to get into law, Rebecca O'Neill started taking classes to pursue this end. She says, "Mind you, at the time, I was over thirty, and I didn't even have an associate's degree. I felt successful every day that I was a family law attorney, because I was helping people who were in emotional turmoil and experiencing a 'bottom' in their lives." Although Rebecca went back to school and earned her degrees later in life than most of the other people in this book, she knew she could do it and that she would be successful in college and in her career. She graduated from the University of Florida, achieved excellent grades, and is now an in-house attorney for a large healthcare organization.

Dr. Dennis Deaton, one of my favorite authors and speakers, teaches that "you alter your destiny by altering your thoughts." How true this has been in my life! The more I think of myself as successful, the more successful I become. This is also true for all those interviewed for this book. It will also be true for you.

2. Practice daily personal affirmations.

In order to believe in yourself, you need to train your subconscious mind. Many of us have conditioned our subconscious minds in the past to believe that we are less than what we are. The subconscious mind does not think for itself; therefore, it believes whatever is fed into it. If it hears negative comments, it believes them. If it hears positive comments, it believes them. Unfortunately, most of us hear, and pay attention to, many more negative comments than positive ones. This is why positive affirmations are so necessary. We need to train and retrain our subconscious minds by feeding them positive thoughts. The subconscious mind does not think, reason, or create. It merely reacts to the thoughts of the conscious mind.

The conscious mind dominates the subconscious mind with dominant thought. World-renowned motivational speaker Earl Nightingale said, "We must control our thinking. The same rule that can lead us to a life of success, wealth, happiness and all the things we have ever dreamed of . . . that very same law can lead us into the gutter."

In *The Intuitive Manager*, author Roy Rowen writes, "Male or female, top brass or lowly trainee, the decision-maker needs to understand how the brain constantly delves into the subconscious to retrieve buried fragments of knowledge and experience, which it then instantaneously fuses with new information."

In *Brain Building*, Marilyn vos Savant, says, "Just as the human body can be strengthened and toned to muscular power through . . . exercise, so too can the mind be strengthened and sharpened. You can't build a great body in a few hours; the same goes for your intellect. Remember that the secret to the success of any exercise program is repetition, repetition, repetition. Only then will you begin to see results."

The subconscious mind can be your ally in building your self-confidence. It can help you to believe in yourself, to believe in your abilities and your potential. But you need to train the subconscious mind and to be diligent in this training. Repeated affirmations, over an extended period of time, will contribute greatly to this training program.

I once participated in a class where the students were asked to select three adjectives that would describe themselves. We were instructed to not think or reason, but just to recite the first three positive adjectives that came into our heads. The first three that entered my mind were "confident, committed, and powerful." I doubt whether the adjectives would have been the same back in the days when I needed to be coerced to visit the Civil Service office to review my test results. I had come a long way since then, but I still didn't realize that I thought of myself as confident and powerful. As I reflected on these words, I knew they were true; however, I needed to keep reminding my subconscious of this. I began, several times each day, to repeat the phrase, "I am a confident, committed, powerful woman." I repeated it to myself whenever I was to give a presentation to a large group, whenever I was walking into a meeting with our company's top management, whenever I needed to handle a difficult employee situation, whenever I was preparing a new lesson for a college class I was teaching, and whenever I was in a situation where I might have previously lacked confidence. I repeated it when I was driving in traffic, as I waited in a supermarket line, when I woke up in the morning, and when I went to bed at night. Because my subconscious mind heard this phrase so often, it became part of my personal belief system. The phrase "I am a confident, committed, powerful woman" has helped me to enjoy more success than I had previously thought possible. I still think of myself with these three adjectives, plus one other—"caring." To this date, I often remind myself that I am a confident, committed, powerful, caring woman.

Affirmations are different for different people, and each of us needs to determine the affirmations that are best for us. Following are some examples that students have shared with me:

- I am a successful student.
- I am capable of excelling in college.
- I have greatness in me.
- I am creating and achieving my dreams.
- I am terrific!

Your affirmations do not have to be long. In fact, shorter ones tend to be easier to remember. You'll want to have some that relate to your personal goals in school and in life. Notice that the above affirmations are all in the present tense. This is important, because the subconscious mind operates only in the present.

It is important to recite your affirmations to yourself several times each day. As you do this, you will be training your subconscious mind. Dr. Napoleon Hill, author of *Think and Grow Rich*, said, "Whatever the mind can conceive and believe, the mind can achieve."

3. Emulate self-confident people.

Who is it you admire most? Most likely, this person possesses much self-confidence. What are the characteristics of this person that you may want to emulate? Regardless of who this person is, you can be selective in the characteristics you choose. In fact, you might select different characteristics from different people, and emulate only those characteristics you admire most.

We can learn much by observing self-confident people. How do they dress? How do they walk and talk? What is their posture? When do they stand? When do they sit? How do they enter a conversation? How do they start a conversation? How do they participate in classroom discussions? Do they seem to "think on their feet"?

Other ways to learn to emulate the characteristics we admire in self-confident, successful people are to talk with them and to ask for their advice. Most people love to hear that others admire them, and they enjoy sharing their wisdom, experience, and advice. A caution, however, is to consciously listen to what they have to say and be willing to take action based on the advice you request.

As you continue to observe self-confident people, you might want to make a list of the characteristics that you most admire about each person. You can then form a list of characteristics you most want to emulate. These would be the characteristics that would help you most in enhancing your self-confidence. The next step would be to determine how you are going to integrate these characteristics into your own personal style. Again, remember that you do not need to be exactly like someone else to be a confident, successful person. The beauty of this is that we can each have our own style and still enjoy all the success we desire in life.

4. Reward yourself for each success.

In a world where we have been raised to be modest and to not "blow our own horns," it is often difficult to accept praise or even to admit that we are successful. How often have you complimented someone on an achievement and received a response such as, "Oh, it was nothing"?

When I interviewed people for my first book, I started by telling them that I considered them to be successful. I followed up by asking if they agreed with my statement. All of the interviewees agreed. If they hadn't, the interview would have ended at that point. In order to be successful, a person needs to have enough self-confidence to admit to others that he/she is successful. This does not mean that you need to brag about this, but rather that you recognize yourself for this success.

Recognition contributes to self-confidence, and we can't depend on others to give us this recognition. Genuine success comes from within. It is self-generated. It is the realization that we are accomplishing our goals and our mission in life. Each of us measures our own success on our own yardstick. As we do this, we need to generate our own recognition.

As we give recognition to ourselves for our accomplishments, we expand our enthusiasm and energy to accomplish more. As we are recognized, our self-confidence grows. Self-confidence breeds more self-confidence, which breeds more success. As we continue to reward ourselves for our successes, the cycle continues.

The type of success you reward is up to you. I can reward myself for writing five pages of this book by taking a break to go for a walk in the park, by treating myself to an ice cream cone, or by making a phone call to a friend. When I finish a chapter, I might celebrate by going to dinner or to the theater with my husband. When the book is published, I will reward myself with a trip to Europe.

The type of reward is also up to you. It might be as simple as a trip to the gym or reading a new best-selling novel. What is important is that you recognize yourself for achieving a goal. As you recognize yourself more, you will achieve more goals, and your confidence in yourself will grow.

5. Surround yourself with positive people.

Olympic champion Wilma Rudolph was the twentieth of twenty-two children in her family. Weak and frail as a child, she contracted pneumonia, scarlet fever, and polio. As a result, her doctors had little hope that she would ever be able to walk. With the encouragement of her mother, Wilma worked at taking one step and then another until, at age eleven, she was able to make it from one side of her yard to the other. When she started high school, she made the basketball team and became one of the starting players when she was a senior. With much hard work, determination, and more encouragement from her mother, she continued to improve her athletic abilities. At the Rome Olympic Games in 1960, she won three gold medals, set world records in both the 100-meter dash and the 200-meter dash, and ran the anchor leg in the four-by-one-hundred-meter relay. She was called the fastest woman on earth. When asked how she had overcome her disability, she responded, "The doctors said I would never walk. My mother said I would. I believed my mother."

Not all of us have had the opportunity to live most of our life with positive people, with people who encourage us, with people who do not criticize us. However, as a college student and as an adult, you can choose the people with whom you spend most of your time.

Have you ever noticed the group dynamics when one person in the group makes a negative statement and another person adds to this negativity? At this point, it is tempting for the others in the group to become negative. The next time this happens in your life, you might want to think about how you feel during this conversation and afterward. Then contrast these feelings with the ones that you have during and after a positive conversation. You will definitely notice a difference. You will feel much better during and after the positive conversations.

As you include more positive people in your circle of friends, you will become more positive. As you become more positive, you will attract more positive people. As you attract more positive people into your life, your self-confidence will grow. As your self-confidence grows, others will also have more confidence in you.

Jill Lublin, who graduated from Wayne State University and is the best-selling author of *Guerrilla Publicity* and *Networking Magic*, adds that your positive friends will give you what you need to move forward and will help you with resources. She says, "When you share your goals with positive people, you'll find that more people want to help you. Because you believe in yourself, they will believe in you."

6. Look and feel your best.

Many students have told me that they would feel better about themselves if they were better looking or, at least, more attractive. They feel that their nose is too large, their hair is too thin, their feet are too big, etc.

The truth is that very few people in this world have beautiful or handsome faces and perfect bodies, and many people who do have beautiful or handsome faces and perfect bodies also have a poor self-image. The difference, for many of us, is that we feel better about ourselves when we look our best. Following are some tips from successful people on looking and feeling your best:

- Wear clothes that are appropriate for the occasion. These clothes do not have to be expensive, but they should fit well and be clean and pressed.
- Practice good grooming habits at all times.
- Wear your hair in a style that looks best on you.
- Stand and sit straight.
- Get enough sleep to look and feel good. I know this is difficult while you are in college, but force yourself to do it, anyway. Let your body tell you how much sleep you need, and make this a priority. When you are well-rested, you'll be amazed at how much more productive you can be.
- Maintain good health. See your doctor when you are ill, and have regular physical checkups.
- Stay physically fit. Aerobic exercises will help, especially walking and swimming.
- Wear a smile. You will soon notice that this will help to attract more positive people into your life. The person who wrote the lyrics, "When you're smiling, the whole world smiles with you," was definitely right!

The better you look, the better you'll feel about yourself. Most people who practice these simple tips for two weeks begin to notice a difference. As people notice a difference, they make a habit of practicing these tips. As these positive habits are formed, your self-confidence will increase.

7. Fake it until you make it.

This is the only place in this book where you will be advised to fake anything. Personal integrity is most important to me, and I believe that honesty is critical to success. What I am recommending here is that you act as if you believe in yourself. By acting self-confident, most people begin to realize that they can be self-confident.

I once took a class to help build my self-confidence. One class exercise was to go to a shopping mall, introduce yourself to a stranger, and engage in a conversation with this stranger. Sales personnel in the mall did not count for points. If we were able to dine with the stranger, we were given extra credit. Since I was quite shy at the time, this was an extremely scary challenge for me. I hesitated and procrastinated. Finally, when I had just one hour left before I had to be back in class, I went into a fast food restaurant within the mall. I ordered my food and looked for someone with a friendly face. When I finally spotted her, I noticed an empty table next to hers. I stood tall while waiting for my food, walked tall to the empty table, and sat tall once I arrived at the table. It was good to sit down, because my knees were shaking. I looked at her, smiled, and asked a question about one of the stores in the mall. Fortunately, she carried the ball from there. She seemed to have a lot of self-confidence. I acted like I did, also. I moved to her table and got the extra points, but I learned that the points for doing this were worth much less than the lesson that I learned and the friend that I gained that day. She later told me that she was impressed with my self-confidence!

Sometimes we have to put ourselves into uncomfortable situations in order to gain confidence in ourselves. When I started working for 3M, my top fear was the fact that I might have to speak in public at some time. Research indicates that this is the number one fear for people in general. I knew that, in order to achieve my goals, I would need to become a good public speaker. This was a paradox for me. To overcome this fear, I joined a Toastmasters club. My first speech was just seven minutes long. It was about myself, a topic that required no research. I practiced until I could deliver this speech flawlessly. When it came time to give the speech, I consciously tried to demonstrate self-confidence; however, my knees shook, and my voice sounded like I was crying. I didn't remember ever before having been as nervous as I was when I gave this speech. However, I tried to demonstrate all of the self-confidence I thought I lacked. As I gave more speeches, my confidence grew to the point that public speaking soon became one of my favorite things to do.

If you think of yourself as successful, you are successful. If you believe in yourself, others will also believe in you. By demonstrating self-confidence, even if you don't think you have it, you will become more self-confident.

8. Affirm those around you.

There are not many people in the world who can't benefit from more self-confidence. I have learned that even the most arrogant and seemingly self-assured people often lack the inner confidence needed to really feel good about themselves. Even these people need compliments. However, when affirming and complimenting people, it is important to be genuine and honest.

The universe is connected. It took me many years to appreciate the saying, "What goes around, comes around." If we are looking for recognition and confidence, we need to recognize and have confidence in others. In business, the most confident executives and managers I know are the ones who give credit to their people who do the work. In school, I've noticed that the genuinely self-confident students are the ones who respect and praise others. In life, the most confident people are the ones who demonstrate confidence in others.

* * * * *

When I interviewed Rita for a management position a few years ago, I found myself wishing more people could be like her. She exhibited more self-confidence than almost anyone would feel in this type of situation. When she walked into my office, she created a good first impression even before any words were spoken. Her posture was erect, her grooming was impeccable, and she was dressed appropriately and professionally. She was well prepared for the interview, answering my questions with much knowledge and professionalism. She also asked some good questions herself. At the end of the interview, she referred to some notes and told me that the information I had given her fit the criteria she had specified for her next job. She reviewed these criteria with me, along with her qualifications for the position. Although I had scheduled eleven additional interviews for this position, I knew immediately that Rita, who was the first interviewee, would be a top candidate.

A year after Rita moved into my department, I sponsored a

"power goaling" workshop for all employees in the department. Rita was eager to review her power goal with me the following week. Once again, she was aspiring to greatness and had developed an action plan to achieve her next major goal in life. To my surprise, she had some questions regarding her potential to reach this goal. Because she shared these concerns with me, I shared with her my own prior experiences with low self-confidence and gave her some suggestions for moving forward.

The next day, Rita hand-delivered to my office a note that I will cherish forever. In the note, she had written: "Thank you very much for the insight you provided yesterday by sharing your story. There are so many mini-lessons I learned that have been running through my mind, especially that confidence can be learned!"

Indeed, self-confidence can be learned. Self-esteem can be developed. The first step is to believe in yourself. I had learned this lesson and was able to convey it to Rita and to others. My intent is that you will also benefit from these shared experiences and incorporate these principles into your life.

Chapter Two

Dare to Dream!

Visualize your reality

"We alter our destiny by altering our thoughts," Dr. Dennis Deaton stated emphatically as he stood in front of his audience of more than 100 students and looked directly at me. "If we will master the power of our minds, we may do or be whatsoever we will." It was February 1994, and I was attending the course on Visioneering that Dr. Deaton had developed and taught through the human potential development company that he had founded. I had learned about the power of visualization two years earlier, and I was convinced that it was a strong factor in putting me on the fast track to creating an ideal life for myself. I decided now was the time to speed up the pace.

Using the Visioneering process, which includes visualizing sensory-rich, emotion-laden images, I began to create my next position at 3M through visualization. I had often said that I would like to have an international assignment, to have the opportunity to live and work outside of the United States. By this time, i knew that just talking about it was not going to make it happen. I needed to start by visualizing my desires and to put these desires in pictures that my subconscious mind could understand in order for it to begin its work. I later wrote the following description of this initial visualization:

> *On Saturday, October 1, 1994, I see Cliff (my husband) and I arriving in our new red Audi 100 at the home we have selected in Brussels, Belgium, where we will be living for the next two years. This is the beginning of my new assignment as 3M's European sales and marketing productivity manager, a position that I have worked toward for the past eleven years.*
>
> *It is a warm autumn day. The sun is shining brightly in the clear blue sky, and the leaves on the trees have started to turn red and gold. In front of us is our new home, which is brown brick with white trim and a pointed roof. Its two-car garage is waiting for the Audi, which is a company car, and also for the second car that we will purchase later this month.*
>
> *I am excited about this excellent opportunity to not only increase the company's sales and marketing effectiveness in Europe and enhance my career, but also to see and experience much of Europe, including the Vatican and the Leaning Tower of Pisa in Italy, the Eiffel Tower and the Louvre in Paris, the theater in London, the green rolling landscape of Ireland, the Alps, ancient cathedrals and museums.*
>
> *Cliff and I look forward to making new acquaintances with the many Europeans that we will meet in the next two years. We are also eager to host many of our American friends and relatives in Europe.*

I repeated the visualization process at least twice each day for several weeks. As I did this, the vision expanded to include the sounds of people speaking English in different accents. It also included aromas, such as those of Belgian waffles and French perfume. As I was able to see my goals more clearly, the original vision was altered until it reached the point where I knew it was what I really wanted. The rest was easy. My vision became a reality before the end of the year. The fantastic results of this visualization process are described later in this chapter. First, let's review the results of several other visualizations, the steps in the visualization process, and how visualization can contribute to your success in college and in the world.

I had first practiced visualization two years earlier while participating in a course facilitated by Dr. Dean Portinga. The course had been developed by his wife, Dr. Bobbie Stevens, who had developed a process for creating an ideal life for herself. Dr. Stevens and Dr. Portinga (or Bobbie and Dean, as they prefer to be called) had founded Unlimited Futures, a company that provides programs for the development of human potential for both individuals and corporations. Bobbie had come to the realization that there are some basic principles of life that govern all that is created. One of these principles is that mental energy directs physical energy. "This is how we create experiences in our lives," she says. "We create our own experiences through our own thoughts or, more accurately, through our deepest beliefs."

Dr. Dennis Deaton agrees with this. In *The Book on Mind Management*, he writes, "We think, and with those thoughts, we create. We create the world we live in. It goes beyond influencing, shaping, or guiding. You and I, in very literal terms, determine what we experience and what we enact into the world. We establish our own happiness or misery, abundance or scarcity . . . We harvest in life, only and exactly, what we sow in our minds."

Bobbie Stevens was sure that she could create whatever she desired in her life. She began by experimenting at the material level. She visualized the townhouse, car, and piano that she wanted to own. She also visualized her job selling real estate to pay for these things. She truly believed that these things would manifest in her life, and they did. She went on to visualize bigger and better material things, and they all manifested. When I met Bobbie, she and her husband owned and lived in a fabulous 7,000-square-foot house, which was on a lake and had a waterfall and trees in the foyer, a swimming pool, and a tennis court.

In themselves, the material things were nice to have, but Bobbie did not stop at that. There were nonmaterial things that were much more important to her. She visualized some higher education and now has two Ph.D. degrees. She visualized a strong spirituality, and she and her husband now teach spirituality courses throughout the United States. Perhaps the most important of her visualizations was when she decided to use the process to attract someone into her life that would be perfectly suited to her in every way.

"If he was perfectly suited for a relationship with me, where we could share our work and life together, what would he be like?" she asked herself. "First, he would have some knowledge about the kinds of things I am now working with, plus a strong interest in this field. He should probably be a psychologist. It would also be good if he had some business background. Of course, he would be intelligent and good-looking. He would also be fun to be with. I can get pretty focused on work, so he should like fun things in order to help me stay light. He would also be curious, an explorer. He would enjoy handling some details, like vacations. He would be very supportive and easy to live with. He would be thoughtful and considerate. We would love each other deeply, and he would appreciate me for being who I am. It would be a very special relationship, and everyone we meet would be inspired by it."

Bobbie worked on enhancing her vision and knew that it would manifest in time. Of course, it did. A short time later, she met Dean Portinga at a retreat, and he is exactly what she had described. They have been married for more than twenty-five years and have since shared the process of visualization with thousands of students. They are an example of what they teach, and their relationship is indeed inspiring.

At the time I participated in Bobbie and Dean's course, I had been dating my husband, Cliff, for about ten months. I knew I loved Cliff, and I enjoyed his company. However, the relationship seemed like it was going nowhere. Cliff had had a heart attack shortly after I met him, and I lived in fear that I might lose him someday. I had a good management position at 3M, but it also seemed that my career had become stagnant. I had a good life, but I wanted it to be better and didn't know how to make it better.

When a business associate mentioned that Bobbie and Dean's course was the best he had ever taken, I was eager to learn more about it. Cliff and I both attended an orientation to learn more about the course. During the orientation, my dominant left brain kept telling me that this is crazy, and it won't work. However, it was evident what the process had done for Bobbie and Dean, and they seemed like such sincere people. Also, my associate, who recommended the course, was a left-brain person, much like myself. My biggest surprise was that Cliff believed everything that Bobbie and Dean were saying. Because Cliff is a chiropractor, he understood completely how mental energy directs physical energy. After a week of discussion, we both decided to participate in the course.

In the beginning of the course, I was still very skeptical. I think Dean could perceive this when he started with a quote from Albert Einstein, "Imagination is more important than knowledge." I decided that, if this was good enough for Albert Einstein, it was good enough for me. I would, at least, pay attention.

Before the first visualization exercise, Dean asked us to write seven choices we would like to manifest in our lives, starting with the words, "I choose." I wrote the following:

1. I choose to sell my house and build my dream home.
2. I choose to own a new Lexus or Acura.
3. I choose friendships with enthusiastic, energetic, intelligent, caring people.
4. I choose a close relationship with a caring husband, who is my soul mate.
5. I choose closer relationships with my children.
6. I choose to be promoted at work into a position having more responsibility.
7. I choose to be more spiritual and more caring.

Our next step was to close our eyes and visualize what each of these choices would look like in our lives, but we didn't stop there. We learned that visualization works best when we act as if our vision has already happened. We went back to our seven choices and changed "I choose" to "I have." Visualization was difficult for me at first, but it began to get easier as I did it more often. Of these original seven choices, I was able to manifest the following in my life:

1. I have sold my house and am building my dream home. At the time I participated in this course, my house had been for sale for several months, and I had received no offers. I had bought a lot on a beautiful pond, and I needed to sell my house in order to start building. I visualized an immediate sale of my home to cash buyers who wanted to close and move in immediately. The following week, I received a cash offer! The buyers wanted to close in nine days and to move in on the day of closing. This was my first experience with visualization, and it was almost spooky! I put most of my belongings into storage and moved to an apartment temporarily while the dream home was being built.

2. I have a new Lexus or Acura.
    This one was easy. I was soon driving a new Acura—a beautiful car!

3. I have friendships with enthusiastic, energetic, intelligent, caring people.
    I am particularly blessed in this area. This world is full of beautiful people, and many of these are my closest friends. Each year, I am fortunate to expand my circle of friends as I meet more enthusiastic, energetic, intelligent, caring people.

4. I have a close relationship with a caring husband, who is my soul mate.
    During the class, Cliff and I shared our feelings about each other with the other participants. I felt he was avoiding me at times. He thought I worried too much. I admit-

ted that I had a fear of him having another heart attack. Dean suggested that we all visualize Cliff as being healthy. I found that when I visualized Cliff as being healthy, it eliminated my fears. When I stopped worrying, he stopped avoiding me. Our relationship began to grow closer, and he proposed later that year. We have an excellent marriage, one that I would not have dreamed possible before I started taking charge of my dreams and visions.

5. I have closer relationships with my children.
    At the time, my son Bryan was twenty-five and my daughter Shelley was nineteen. Although we were close, I knew that we could be closer. As time goes on, the three of us continue to be a close family. This was exemplified later at a party that 3M gave in my honor. Shelley asked the party planners if she could speak during the program portion of the celebration. She gave a tribute that would cause any mother to beam with pride. She ended by saying, "She is not only my mother. She is my friend, confidant, and mentor." Afterward, Bryan told his grandmother that he was so proud of his sister that it brought tears to his eyes.

6. I have been promoted at work into a position having more responsibility.
    Three months later, a new vice president transferred into my business unit. I immediately wrote him a letter describing the position I had created during the visualization process. Within a month, he appointed me to this position. I received three additional promotions in the next five years.

7. I am more spiritual and more caring.
    This is one that I continue to work on. Spirituality is extremely important to me. People are extremely important to me. I pray every night that I will remember this in everything I do the following day.

* * * * *

Visualization was one of the critical steps in the process taught in this course. By the time I completed the course, I felt like I was walking on clouds. I was a firm believer in the power of visualization.

What would you like to create in your life? Do you want to have better grades? Do you aspire to become a better team player? Do you wish to have more close friends? Do you dream of excelling at a future career?

Do you engage in visualization? Of course, you have dreams. I have never met a person without dreams. But do you have a structured program to make these dreams come true? Walt Disney said, "If you can dream it, you can do it."

Henry David Thoreau said, "If one advances confidently in the direction of his dreams, and endeavors to live the life which he has imagined, he will meet with success unexpected in common hours."

Jill Lublin is a person who has advanced confidently in the direction of her dreams and has met with success. For a long time, Jill had dreamed of writing a book and having it published. She visualized her book listed on the best-seller list. She also visualized herself giving speeches about her book after it was published. Her dream started coming true when she was asked to co-author a book called *Guerrilla Publicity*. How exciting it was when she began to see her book on the shelves of bookstores! It was even more exciting when her book became a best seller just four weeks after it was published.

Jill did not stop visualizing her success once her dream had come true. Her next dream to come true was a second book, *Networking Magic*, which was ranked number one on BarnesandNoble.com just two weeks after it was published. Jill is now an international professional speaker and is the host of a syndicated radio show called *Do the Dream*. As this book goes to print, she is also piloting a television show called *GoodNews TV*. While she makes her dreams come true, she also helps others to make their dreams come true.

In *You'll See It When You Believe It*, Dr. Wayne Dyer says, "Your determination to succeed is nothing more than your thought to do so. The idea of success is really the thought of success." In this book, he shares that his thoughts had always created his world. He described his visualization process at age thirteen. He spent many nights watching *The Tonight Show* on a tiny black-and-white television. He pictured himself as a guest on *The Tonight Show* and, in his mind, practiced talking with the host, Steve Allen. He would actually work on routines, as he imagined himself being a guest on the show. In his mind's picture, he was an adult appearing on the show and discussing the things he knew to be true. Even then, he visualized himself telling *The Tonight Show* audience that we are able to choose our own destinies.

Dr. Dyer wrote *Your Erroneous Zones* while he was teaching at a university. He struggled for almost a year with the thought that he needed to go out on his own and leave the security of a bimonthly paycheck. "I had wonderful pictures in my mind's eye," he said. "I saw myself talking to everyone in America about the ideas I had just finished writing about in *Your Erroneous Zones*. I could see in my mind that the book was going to be very successful." He left his university position and began working his plan to follow his dreams. As negative people told him that he could not accomplish his vision, he became even more committed.

A year later, his book was on the *New York Times* best-seller list. His vision had begun to manifest! Within a few months, the book was at the top of the list, where it stayed for almost two years. Then one day, he received the "magic phone call," which was to lead to the fulfillment of the image that he had had since he was thirteen years old. He appeared on *The Tonight Show* three times within an eleven-day period.

In *You'll See it When You Believe It*, he states, "[*Your Erroneous Zones*] was eventually published in twenty-six languages around the world. Other books have followed, as have tapes, articles, international travel for professional speaking engagements, and an opportunity for me to make a difference in the lives of millions and millions of people. I received more money in the first year I was on my own without the security of a regular paycheck than I had in the entire thirty-six years of my life before then."

When Michael Norwood was in his teens, he visualized himself on the *Merv Griffin Show* talking about his success as a writer. Although he did not appear on the *Merv Griffin Show* before it went off the air, he later realized that his true vision is that he is a famous author appearing on a national television show. In our interview, he said, "It is now more tangible to me that I will be on *Oprah* and other major television shows." He has also been a guest on more than 300 radio shows.

Visualization is not new. It has been used since the beginning of time. Aristotle said that the soul cannot think without pictures. "The reasoning mind thinks in the form of images . . . As the mind determines the objects it should pursue or avoid in terms of these images, even in the absence of sensation, it is stimulated to action when occupied with them."

In more recent times, Conrad Hilton created mental pictures of owning a hotel before having one. Ray Kroc, the founder of McDonald's, wrote in *Grinding It Out: The Making of McDonald's* that he used mental images to create his goals. Visualization is the most widely used mental tool in modern sports. Mike Powell, who has held the world record in the long jump, would picture his record jump as he would jump from his kitchen through the dining room into the den over the green shag carpeting and land in front of his mother's red leather easy chair. He was in second place in Tokyo when his vision came back to him. He later said, "As I stare at the horizon, at the peak of my jump, I think I see, just for a second, my mom's red leather easy chair at the end of the pit."

Lois Crandell, who is now retired from her position as CEO of a large San Diego based medical device company, knew the meaning of struggle and hardship as a child. The oldest of ten children, she grew up on a farm in rural Minnesota. When she was three years old, her younger sister died in a fire that destroyed their farmhouse. Her mother, who had been burned over 80 percent of her body, spent several months in the hospital before she recovered and returned to her family.

Lois had many chores on the farm, which included cooking for the family at age eight, driving a tractor by the age of nine, and helping with the younger siblings. She dreamed of finishing college and living by the ocean. While reading *The Strangest Secret* by Earl Nightingale, she realized how important visualization would be in order to make her dreams come true. She read the words, "We must control our thinking. The same rule that can lead us to a life of success, wealth, happiness and all the things we have ever dreamed of . . . that very same law can lead us into the gutter. It's all in how we use it . . . for good or for bad. This is the strangest secret in the world."

After reading about visualization and success, Lois wrote ten goals and visualized the achievement of these goals each day for a year. She has achieved all ten of these goals, which included an excellent marital relationship, running a venture company and taking it public, and living in California. As she visualized, she thought of Earl Nightingale's statement about a person becoming what he thinks about. "When I would close my eyes and see these visualization scenarios, I would actually see the Pacific Ocean from a dwelling high above it," she said. "I now live in a condo, which overlooks Mission Bay. On a clear day, I can see the Pacific Ocean. As I sit in my favorite spot, that old visualization comes back to me."

At age twenty, Christina Gerrish is a full-time college student. Although she also works full time, her grades are excellent. She says that visualizing herself as successful helps her to stay focused on what she needs to get done.

Lois and Christina are strong believers in the power of visualization. So is Arnold Schwarzenegger, who said, "The key to success is to create a vision of who you want to be, and then picture it as if it has already happened." In 1976, a sports reporter asked Arnold what he was going to do, now that he had retired from bodybuilding. The reporter was startled by the answer. "I am going to be the number-one-box-office star in all of Hollywood," he said. As the reporter wondered how this man with the thick Austrian accent and monstrous build could become a box-office star, Arnold explained that he would use the same visualization process that helped him to become very successful at bodybuilding. Arnold had created his vision of being a very successful actor, just as he had created his vision of being a very successful bodybuilder. The rest is history. He became the successful actor of his dreams and later became a successful candidate for governor of California. It all started with a dream.

Are you visualizing your success in college and in life? If so, great! If not, let's get started. Now that you've read some examples of how visualization has affected the lives of successful people, it's time to make this process work for you. As you learn more about the visualization process from different specialists in this field, you will see that the steps in the process can vary. Although you will want to use the process that works best for you, it's important to remember that each of the various processes focus on creating mental pictures in the *present tense*. The following process has created success for students, athletes, and business professionals.

1. Determine what you want to create in your life.

What do you really want in life? What does success mean to you? What will you commit to achieving? We'll spend more time clarifying your desires in a later chapter, but now you should have an idea of what you would like to create in your life. When determining this, be sure to take into consideration all aspects of your life. Include such factors as relationships, health, school, future career, material wants and needs, spiritual growth, and anything else that is important to you. Make a written list of these things. Be sure to write the *result* of what you wish to create, not *how* you plan to get it. Read your list to make sure that these are the things you want to create. Lois Crandell says, "Be careful what you visualize, because you will get it!"

Next, review your list to make sure that it is in the present tense. When you visualize, your subconscious mind will be working in the present tense. Also, make sure that you have written what you want, not what you don't want. When you visualize, you'll need to concentrate on what you want. For example, if you are overweight, don't write that you want to lose weight. Your subconscious mind will focus on the word *weight*, rather than the fact that you want a thinner, healthier, more-attractive body. In this case, you might want to write, "I am physically healthy and attractive."

Now review your list again. Have you written the desired results of what you want to create, rather than how you will create it? Are the items in the list in the present tense? Are the items stated as the results you want, rather than as the results you don't want? Are they really what you want, rather than the things you think you *should* want? Do all of the items in your list excite you? Cross out the ones that do not excite you.

By now, you have probably written, crossed out, and rewritten several of the items on your list. Look at the list one more time. Are you making choices for other people in any of the items on your list? If so, you will want to reword these. For example, you can choose the kind of relationship you want, but don't name the other person in that relationship. That person will need to make his or her own choices. Ensure that none of the items conflict with each other. Also, you will want to make sure that the items on your list do not cause harmful effects to another person.

2. Eliminate distractions.

Distractions come in two varieties: internal and external. You can have control over both. First, you will want to eliminate the external distractions. Go to a quiet place where you will not be interrupted. Some people have the advantage of a convenient, serene forest, lakeside, or mountain setting. For others, it might be a bedroom or even a closet. If there is a telephone in the room, turn off the ringer. If you have a cell phone, turn it off.

The internal distractions are more difficult for most of us to eliminate, but it can be done. We all have so many things on our minds that our thoughts will tend to wander if we do not discipline our minds to stay focused on the task at hand. I recommend engaging in the visualization process while in a sitting position. Most of us can relax while we are sitting, and we're more likely to stay awake when we're sitting rather than lying down.

Close your eyes and give yourself some time to unwind. If your mind wanders onto a trivial matter and you think you must remember it, open your eyes and write it down. Then close your eyes again, stay seated, and unwind.

3. Relax your body and your mind.

Most of us do not realize how much stress and tension is in our body until we start to relax. If you have a favorite relaxation technique, use it now to relax your body before you start visualizing. If you do not have a favorite technique, I suggest the following:

- Now that you are in a sitting position with your eyes closed, let the chair support your body.
- Uncross your legs and feel yourself sink into the chair.
- Take a deep breath, inhaling slowly. Hold your breath. Then slowly exhale as you imagine the tension leaving your body. Repeat this four times, each time becoming more aware of your breathing.
- Let all your muscles relax as much as you can before going through the following steps.
- Tense the muscles of your feet and ankles, curling your toes. Gently release this tension until your feet and ankles are totally relaxed.
- Tense the muscles in the lower part of your legs. Slowly release this tension.
- Tense the muscles in your upper legs. As before, slowly release the tension from your legs. Your legs, ankles, and feet should now be fully relaxed and feel like they are hanging limply.
- Tense your hips and abdomen. As before, let this area of your body relax slowly.

- Tense your chest and back muscles. Slowly, gently relax these muscles.
- Direct your attention to your hands. Quickly make two fists, and slowly relax your hands.
- Bend your wrists. Then relax them.
- Tense the muscles in your lower arms. Slowly let them relax. Do the same with your upper arms.
- Shrug your shoulders. Let them relax. Shrug them a second time, and then let them relax even more. Your arms are now beginning to hang comfortably by your sides.
- Turn your head from side to side as far as it will go. Do this again. Touch your chin to your chest, and then raise it as high as you can. Relax your neck muscles.
- Clench your teeth tightly together. Now relax your jaw muscles. Smile as broadly as you can. Then relax your mouth. Wrinkle your nose. Relax it. Close your eyes tighter. Relax them. Wrinkle your forehead. Relax it, feeling the tension flow out of your head.
- If any muscles in your body are still tense, direct your attention to these muscles. Relax them one-by-one.

Your body should now be totally relaxed. To ensure that your mind is also relaxed, visualize yourself in a quiet, peaceful setting. In Bobbie Stevens and Dean Portinga's course, they suggest visualizing a blue sky with one fluffy white cloud floating above you. You can relax your mind as you direct your attention to this fluffy white cloud. Now, visualize yourself floating high above the earth on this fluffy cloud in the blue sky. As you float on this cloud, let all of the stress and tension leave your mind. This has worked very well for me. Although it's been several years since I took Bobbie and Dean's course, I still think of them every time I see fluffy white clouds in the sky. I also still think of my first attempt at visualization and the wonderful results that I have created in my life from this process.

4. Create a mental movie.

Eleanor Roosevelt said, "The future belongs to those who believe in the beauty of their dreams." As human beings, not only can we dream, but also we can make our dreams come true. You are now ready to start creating your future through visualization and to put yourself on the path to realizing your vision.

At this point, bring one of the choices from your list into your mind. Picture yourself as if you have this in your life. The important word here is *picture*. Visualization works best in pictures, not paragraphs. In *Control Theory*, William Glasser said, "Most people do not know that they are motivated by the pictures in their heads and have no idea of how powerful and specific they are . . . the power of pictures is total . . . and when we change the important pictures, we change our lives."

Dennis Deaton advises visualizing these pictures as sensory-rich, emotion-laden images. He says, "The more sensory-rich and emotion-laden the images, the more powerful they are to the subconscious, the more quickly they are absorbed, and the more readily they are acted upon."

Envision yourself using all of your senses in your mental movie.

- **Sight.** For my position in Europe, I could see the house and the car, as well as the autumn colors in the trees. Lois Crandell could see the Pacific Ocean. We both saw ourselves in decision-making settings where we had a major impact on the growth of our respective businesses. You might see a printed copy of your commencement program, and there are asterisks or the words, *summa cum laude*, next to your name.
- **Hearing.** I could hear the sound of people speaking English in different accents. Lois could hear the waves breaking on the shore. You might hear the ring of a telephone as you visualize receiving a job offer in your chosen field after graduation.
- **Smell.** I could smell French perfume and Belgian waffles. Lois could smell the many fragrant flowers around her dream home by the ocean.
- **Taste.** I could taste the rich Belgian chocolates. Lois could taste the fresh seafood.

- **Touch.** In my vision, I could feel myself holding onto a strap in a European train to support myself as I traveled from one country to another. Lois could feel the wind on her face as she sailed on the ocean. You might feel a football hitting your hands as you catch a pass for the winning touchdown.

William Glasser said, "The way all creatures make contact [with the outside world] is through the senses associated with our eyes, ears, fingers, tongues and noses. But it is important to keep in mind that it is through these same senses that we make contact with our own minds and bodies."

While visualizing, let yourself also concentrate on how you feel emotionally and spiritually. If you are committed to your vision, these feelings will be good. When you have finished your visualization, slowly open your eyes.

5. Reinforce your vision through consistent mental rehearsal.
Your first visualization session might take some time; however, it is time well invested. Future visualization sessions might take anywhere from one to thirty minutes, depending on the circumstances. I recommend that you plan to visualize your goals and dreams at least twice each day and that you keep the end result in your thoughts throughout the day. Through your thoughts, you are creating your life. Your mind will then drive your actions in the direction of your dominant thoughts.

* * * * *

You have seen that visualization has worked in the lives of many successful people. You are probably now wondering how it works and how it differs from daydreaming. In *The Book on Mind Management*, Dr. Dennis Deaton states, "Vision is the element that integrates all of your faculties. When you visualize your goals in sensory-rich, emotion-laden images, you unite conscious mind, subconscious, and the energy and passions of the body into one unified force. The melding of all of your faculties vaults you to the highest attainable levels of human performance." He summarizes the process by the following four steps:

- The conscious mind activates the subconscious mind with the dominant thought.
- The subconscious mind develops plans to realize the dominant thought. It then flashes the plans to the conscious mind for evaluation.
- The conscious mind evaluates and approves the plans.
- The subconscious mind governs the body to bring the plans into working reality.

Other experts have made the following statements on the benefits of visualization:

"When we change the models in our mind, we change the results in our life." (Mark Victor Hansen, co-author of *Chicken Soup for the Soul* series)

"Vividly experienced imagery, imagery which is both seen and felt, can substantially affect the brain waves, blood flow, heart rate, skin temperature, gastric secretions, and immune response . . . in fact the total physiology." (Jean Houston in *The Possible Human*)

"All thoughts which have been emotionalized [given feeling] and mixed with faith, begin immediately to translate themselves into their physical equivalent or counterpart." (Napoleon Hill in *Think and Grow Rich*)

"Your nervous system cannot tell the difference between an imagined experience and a 'real' experience. In either case, it reacts automatically to information which you give it from your forebrain." (Dr. Maxwell Maltz in *Pycho-Cybernetics*)

"Each time you 'see' yourself performing exactly the way you want with perfect form, you physically create neural patterns in your brain." (Kay Porter and Judy Foster in *The Mental Athlete*)

"As long as the mind can envision the fact that you can do something, you can do it. I visualized myself being there already—having achieved the goal already." (Arnold Schwarzenegger)

"We become what we think about all day long." (Ralph Waldo Emerson)

"It has been said that [the] picturing power of the mind is the greatest gift that God has ever given to man. It has the ability to construct images of success before the actual experiences are born. It can paint pictures that will fire our wills and exalt our spirits. This ability to travel ahead of our own success can draw us on with the greatest pleasure towards the most worthwhile objectives." (Sterling W. Sill in *The Upward Reach*)

* * * * *

In a dramatic manner, Dennis Deaton exposes his class participants to the Michelangelo Principle, which is "Masters *see* their creations *before* they are created." The Academia delle Arte houses one of the finest art collections in Europe. The most breathtaking sculpture in this museum is one of Michelangelo's best, the statue of *David*. This sculpture is not only massive, but it is also perfect in every detail. The visitor to the museum sees the muscle definition in the legs, as well as the veins and tendons in the hands, wrists, and feet. When he saw *David*, Dennis had to remind himself that some human being had chipped, chiseled, and carved this figure out of dense, unrelenting marble.

As a result of his visit, Dennis decided to look into the history of the creation of *David*. He learned that, in 1501, the city-state of Florence commissioned Michelangelo to create a giant statue to be positioned in a prominent city square. There existed, at that time, a huge block of white marble that had been severely damaged and thought to be unfit for an average work of art, much less for a masterpiece. Michelangelo studied the block carefully, not only doing abstract mathematical calculations in his head, but also visualizing the end result of his creation. After visualizing *David*, he knew that this was the block he would use. He saw that the flaws did not cut through the figure in the stone. *David* lived so vividly in Michelangelo's mind that he saw his creation in the present tense before he ever even took the chisel into his hand to carve it.

Dr. Deaton's story of the statue of *David* lived so vividly in my mind that I knew I also wanted to see this work of art. I added this to my visualization of my European job. Now, after 500 years, thousands of people are inspired each day by the vision and work of this great master. Many, such as I, are also inspired by the Michelangelo Principle and what it can do in our lives.

In the beginning of this chapter, I reviewed the visualization process that I used to create the experience of living and working in Europe. As I visualized this over the next several weeks, the vision became clearer. I made modifications in my vision as I clarified my goals and desires. The brown house in Belgium became a white stucco house with French shutters in the country outside of Paris, France. The red Audi was changed to a French-made automobile, a Renault top-of-the-line Safrane. I could still smell the Belgian waffles and knew that I wanted to spend at least one day each week in Brussels, attending meetings with Europeans and other Americans and visiting with my brother and sister-in-law who were living there.

In July of that year, I received a phone call from the vice president of 3M Europe. It was exactly as I had visualized it. In fact, I could have written the script for this conversation! He offered me the position and said that they were still trying to determine whether I would be headquartered in Paris or Brussels. In September, we found the perfect house, which had six bedrooms and thirteen bathrooms, in a scenic Paris suburb. We moved there in November, when I started my job as European Marketing and Sales Productivity and Quality Manager. I had offices in both Paris and Brussels and traveled throughout Europe 80 percent of the time. Since our children were grown, my husband Cliff was able to travel with me much of the time. We saw magnificent beauty and history in fourteen European countries, both those included in my vision and others. While accomplishing my business and professional objectives, I made many new European friends and strengthened existing relationships.

One of my most memorable days in Europe was the day that I was able to see the statue of *David* with my own eyes. He is just as magnificent as I had imagined him to be. Again I was reminded that masters see their creations before they are created. How true this had become for me! It will become true for you, also, if you believe in the power of your dreams and invest your energy in that direction.

Chapter Three

Determine Your Priorities!

And live them each day

Throughout much of my adult life, I considered myself one of the biggest victims of the Superwoman Syndrome. I completed two college degrees while working full time and raising two children. This might have been enough to undertake, but I didn't stop there. It was as if I wanted to show the world and myself that I could do it all—and do it perfectly. I made delicious and nutritious meals and kept a spotless house. After finishing the dinner dishes and putting the kids to bed each evening, I would scrub the kitchen floor (on my hands and knees) before doing my schoolwork. People would comment that my basement floor was so clean that they thought they could eat off of it. Weekends were my time to catch up with the things I was not able to accomplish during the week. I often felt guilty for not doing more.

One of the reasons that I was able to be so productive was that I made lists of the things that I needed to do. By following the lists, I didn't need to take the time to think about what to do next. I enumerated the tasks on paper as they came into my head, but I didn't spend much time prioritizing the lists. Since I thought that I had to get all of these things done, the priority didn't seem very important.

I would normally start at the beginning of the list and work my way to the end. However, the lists were usually so long that I rarely got all the way to the end. The remaining items would just be transferred to the next list.

One Friday evening, I made a very long list of the things I wanted to accomplish that weekend. One of the items on my list was to call my grandmother. She was my only living grandparent, and I loved her dearly. She was of Italian descent and one of the best cooks I had ever known. She would often call me at work to tell me that she had made spaghetti sauce and meatballs and would ask if I would stop by after work to take this meal home with me. When I was sick, she would call every day to see how I was feeling. She cared very deeply for each of her children and grandchildren. She gave of herself and expected nothing in return. As I thought of her on this particular Friday evening, I reminded myself that I hadn't talked with her in a while. On my list, I wrote, "Call Grandma." With all of the many things on my list, I never got to this item over the weekend.

I had a late meeting on Monday night, so I added my item to call Grandma to my Tuesday night list. Grandma died suddenly of congestive heart failure on Tuesday. I had never made the phone call. After all of these years, I still often dream about making that call to my grandmother.

The loss of my grandmother taught me a very important lesson in priorities. I had always said my family was my priority, but I didn't live that way. There seemed to be too many things that got in the way, and I procrastinated on the things that were on the top of my priority list.

After my grandmother's death, I started thinking more about the importance of people in my life. I visited my parents more often and wrote notes to people who were important to me. I knew that I cared about people, and I wanted them to know that, too. However, as time went on, the demands of everyday life as I had known it in the past began to take their toll on me. Once again, I allowed myself to be a victim, a person who never seemed to have time for things that did not have worldly deadlines. It took another death, this time of a close friend, to jolt me to the realization of the critical importance of making a commitment to priorities in my life.

My friend's name was Cliff. I had known him since before the days of office cubicles. We worked together as systems analysts. His desk was behind mine, and we shared a telephone. When I first knew him, he was a confirmed bachelor, who partied with his buddies at night and complained about the water in the shower hurting in the morning. Then he met the love of his life—a bright, caring woman named Chris. Cliff and Chris married and had two children, a girl and a boy. They were a perfect American family.

Cliff was an excellent systems analyst and set high standards for his own performance. He was also one of the most ethical people I have ever known. For these reasons, I enjoyed working with him. We often collaborated on projects, even after we moved to different departments within the company. We remained good friends throughout the years, and I most enjoyed when he would talk about his wife and children. I can still picture the smile on his face and the light in his eyes when he spoke of his family.

When Cliff was thirty-nine years old, he was diagnosed with terminal cancer. At first, he requested that he have no visitors, as Chris cared for him at home. When he later came to terms with his prognosis, he and Chris invited friends to take turns visiting him on Fridays during lunchtime. It was decided that two of us would visit each Friday and that we would bring lunch for the family to eat as we spent time with him. Because of my hectic schedule, I postponed my visit to Cliff until three weeks after receiving the invitation.

On the day before my scheduled visit, I awoke from a dream very early in the morning. In my dream, I was visiting Cliff. I was dismayed, because I did not have the lunch with me. When I walked into Cliff's house, the light was so bright that I could hardly open my eyes. I learned later that morning that he had passed away at precisely the time of my dream. When I explained to Chris how sorry I was that I had not seen him before he died, she replied that she had heard of my dream from another friend and that she believed that Cliff had come to say good-bye to me.

It took the deaths of two people, who were close to me, to make me realize how important it is to set priorities in my life. I had often joked that I needed to live at least 1,000 years to accomplish everything I wanted to do in life. Now, I finally understood that I needed to decide what was important to me and to do these things during the limited amount of time available to me on this earth.

Because of the importance of the subject, much has been written and taught on time management, life management, and self-management. However, most people still feel the pressures of too much to do in too little time. There are many reasons for this, one of which is the need for better prioritization.

All of the successful college students and graduates in this book are able to accomplish those things that are important to them in life. They each have established prioritization techniques to help them align their activities with their values. They are able to distinguish between what is important and what is urgent. They focus on the important activities, which deliver value. They fully comprehend what President Dwight Eisenhower meant when he said, "Most things which are urgent are not important, and most things which are important are not urgent."

Many of us complain about interruptions in the course of the day that rob us of time we had planned to spend on the things that are important to us; however, we allow these interruptions to have power over us. We might also say that we have our priorities straight and then demonstrate otherwise through our actions. For example, think about how we use "call waiting" on our telephones. A person could be involved in an important telephone discussion with a close friend, when he hears the call waiting beep on his phone. He immediately puts the close friend on hold while he takes the call from the unknown caller. When I last did this, I reflected on the message that my action might have given to the first person. I also reexamined my values and asked myself if my activities were aligned with them. I reminded myself of a quote from Goethe, who said, "Things which matter most must never be at the mercy of things which matter least."

In *The 7 Habits of Highly Effective People*, Stephen Covey discusses four generations of time management. The first generation is characterized by notes and checklists. Through the years, most of us have learned that it is easier to write things down and to keep checklists than it is to try to remember everything that we think we have to do.

Calendars and appointment books characterize the second generation. This is an attempt to look ahead and to schedule the future. The advent of the day planner has helped to integrate the checklist with the appointment book. This second generation has added some contributions in the area of organization for many people.

The third generation adds the concepts of prioritization, of clarifying values, and of comparing the relative worth of activities based on their relationship to those values. We will spend more time on this later in this chapter.

Covey introduced a fourth generation, which recognizes that "time management" is really a misnomer. He says, "The challenge is not to manage time, but to manage ourselves." He explains that we spend time in one of four ways and that there are two factors that define an activity. These two factors are *urgent* and *important*.

Urgent items require immediate attention, such as a ringing telephone. Urgent matters are usually visible and popular with others. They are often pleasant, easy, and fun to do. However, they are not necessarily a priority and are most often unimportant.

Important items relate to results. If something is important, it contributes to one's mission, values, and/or high-priority goals. Important matters usually require a person to be proactive. If we don't have a clear idea of what is important in our lives, we will often react to the urgent matters and ignore or dismiss those which are important.

According to Covey's model, we spend our time in the following four ways:

1. Activities which are both urgent and important, e.g., deadline-driven projects, such as studying for an exam
2. Activities which are important but not urgent, e.g., relationship building, planning
3. Activities which are urgent but not important, e.g., interruptions
4. Activities which are both not urgent and not important, e.g., trivia, playing games on the computer

If we are managing our priorities, the majority of our time will be spent on those activities that are important and not urgent.

Time Management Exercise

The following exercise will help you determine how you spend your time. For the next two days, keep a list of your activities in either fifteen-minute or thirty-minute segments, whichever works best for you. When you are interrupted, list the nature of the interruption along with the amount of time that it took. At the end of the second day, you will see how you have spent your time and the approximate amount of time you have spent on each of activity. It is particularly useful to do this while you are studying.

When you have finished the time recording, prepare four sheets of paper by labeling the first "Urgent/Important," the second "Important/Not Urgent," the third "Urgent/Not Important," and the fourth "Not Urgent/Not Important." Now transfer your activities from your time recording, along with the time allocations for each, to the appropriate sheets of paper. When you have completed this, ask yourself the following questions:

- Are all the items on the first sheet (Urgent/Important) really important? If not, take time now to transfer these items to the appropriate sheets.
- Are all of the items on the second sheet (Important/Not Urgent) really important? If not, take time now to transfer these items to the appropriate sheets.

- How much of my time am I spending on the activities that are really important to me?
- If I am not spending the majority of my time on the items that are important to me, what can I change in my life in order to do this? This might involve scheduling non-interruptible time for important activities, learning to say no, or just eliminating activities that are not that important to you.

* * * * *

Gayle Crowell is an amazing executive with a big job and an equally big heart. When I met her, she was the CEO of RightPoint, Inc., a company specializing in helping other companies to better understand their customers. As CEO, she led RightPoint from startup status to becoming a $700 million company in less than two years. She is also the mother of six children, a licensed pilot, and a former first-grade and college teacher.

I first met Gayle in Chicago where she was speaking at an e-Commerce conference. Not only was she one of the most knowledgeable speakers in her field at the time, but she also has a speaking style which totally captivates an audience. As soon as she finished her speech, I made my way to the front of the room and asked her if she would be available to speak at a conference that I was hosting for more than 1,000 marketers later in the year. Fortunately, she was available, and this gave me an opportunity to learn more about her.

Gayle and I did not talk with each other between the day we originally met and the day before my conference. She had trained her assistant very well to handle the logistical details concerning her speech at the conference and to ensure that I was comfortable with the arrangement. When I asked her assistant about Gayle's speaker fee, she quoted an amount, told me that the amount was negotiable if it was higher than my budget, and stated that Gayle would like me to contribute this entire speaking fee to a charity, which she named. This was the first time in my entire career that I had hired a speaker or a consultant, who wanted me to donate the money that they earned. Because of my curious nature, I later asked Gayle about this. She responded, "I want to give back in many ways. Since I have been running a startup company and my family is my top priority, I don't have a lot of time. What I do have is money. I really enjoy speaking and helping people to learn. Since I don't have a lot of time to volunteer for specific charities, I have decided that one way to do this is to donate my speaking fees to the charities that I want to impact. Since I don't need the extra money and don't have a way to create more time in a twenty-four-hour day, this is a way that I can contribute. For this chapter of my life, it is a good way to give back."

One of the reasons that Gayle is extremely successful is that she has set priorities in her life and examines her actions based on these priorities. She said, "Being successful is one of those things that encompasses all of your life. At the end of every day, I go through a ritual to reflect on the day and on my life to ensure that my priorities are in order. I feel good about what I have done that day and look for things that I could have done better. When I go to bed at night, I feel good about who I am as a person. Not every day is perfect, of course, but, in general, I'm very satisfied."

Gayle then added, "I set a very high priority on my family. It's not just my family, but people. My priorities include my extended family and many close friends. I have a very strong commitment to my six children in helping to shape their growth and in spending the appropriate amount of time with them. This often is a challenge when you're running a startup company. It's important to have a commitment. With that commitment, I find the execution is fairly easy, because I can then use my organizational skills and whatever else I need to get things in the proper perspective. This is a very strong thing for me. When I have interviewed for jobs during my career, I have always made it a point during the interview process to inform the interviewers that my family is a very high priority for me and that I'm not a person who would sacrifice that. This has worked well for me."

Gayle defines success in terms of feeling good about who we are and the choices we are making. She said, "I think it is important to feel good about a number of aspects of our lives, regardless of the choices we have made in the past. In the fast-paced world in which we live, we sort of get pulled into our career, because it's most pressing with people hammering at us to get things done. But I think it's important to step back and to know that there are many pieces of our lives. Each of us has many roles in life, and we need to define the roles that are most important to us. I believe that we live our lives in chapters. In one chapter, a career may be more important; in another, time with children will be a higher priority." She added that, in order to become successful, a person must define these roles and determine which are most important to her during the current "chapter." It is then much easier to set priorities for a particular chapter in life.

Living our priorities in each chapter of our life is important to success. What are the things that are most important to you during the current chapter of your life as a student?

Many experts in the field of life management advise us to have a personal mission statement and to state what we see as the overall purpose of our life. Your purpose might include spirituality, personal growth and development, relationships, future career, contributions to society, possibly even self-actualization. Your purpose could be simple, or it could be complex. During this chapter of your life, it might be just to be the best student you can possibly be.

Several years ago, when asked to articulate my personal mission statement, without putting a lot of thought in it, I said that my mission was to help others to achieve their dreams. This is still one of my top priorities. If you have not yet defined your purpose, I would suggest that you spend some time thinking about this during the next few days. It will then be easier to set priorities and to accomplish related tasks.

Whether or not you have clearly defined your personal mission statement, you can still determine your priorities. The following steps have worked for many successful students, and they will work for you.

1. Determine your true values.

If you were asked to develop a list of your values right now, would they be your honest values, or would they be a list of values you think you should have? Keep this question in mind as you engage in this exercise.

Start by making a list of items that you value most in life. Your value list might include some of the following:

- Relationship with family members
- Relationship with significant other
- Dedication to learning
- Excellent grades
- Spirituality
- Health and physical fitness
- Close friendships with like-minded people
- Rewarding and exciting future career
- Sports and recreation
- Personal development and growth
- Travel
- Community or church service
- Talent development
- Hobby and leisure activities

Your list might also include some of your personal values that are not listed above.

2. Prioritize your value list.

During this exercise, you will be working with your top seven values, just because it becomes extremely difficult to work with more than seven. If you have listed more than seven, you can use the following method to decrease the number to seven.

1. Determine whether any of your values have similar meanings. If so, combine them into one value statement.
2. If you have seven or fewer values on your list, go to number 10.
3. If you have more than fourteen values on your list, cross out the ones that are least important to you until you have just fourteen (or fewer) items remaining on the list.

4. Find the top value from your list, and put an asterisk in front of it.

5. Now find your lowest-priority value, and cross it out.

6. If you now have just seven values on your list, go to number 10.

7. Find your next highest value. Put an asterisk in front of it.

8. From the remaining list, find the value that now has the lowest priority on the list. Cross it out.

9. If you still have more than seven values remaining on your list, go back to number 7. Otherwise, continue by going to number 10.

10. From this exercise, you should now have a list of your top values. If you so desire, you can prioritize these values using the same method. To do this, write the number "1" in front of your top value. Then write the number "7" in front of the lowest value on this list (if you have seven values listed). Next, write the number "2" in front of your highest of the remaining values on your list, write the number "6" in front of the lowest of the remaining values, and so forth. If you have fewer than seven values listed, you can make the necessary adjustments to these instructions. For many people, this process of selection and elimination works better than just trying to select first, second, and third priorities in sequence. The major result is that this will help you to determine which of the many activities on your daily "to do" list best fits within your value system and are, therefore, your highest priorities.

3. Plan and prioritize your activities.

Victor Hugo said, "He who every morning plans the transaction of the day and follows out that plan, carries a thread that will guide him through the maze of the most busy life. But where no plan is laid, where the disposal of time is surrendered merely to the chance of incidence, chaos will soon reign."

As Stephen Covey noted, most of us develop checklists. This is the first step toward prioritization of our activities. Although it is important to develop action lists for each day, some people prefer to work from a master list, which feeds their daily lists. Before I moved to Europe, I had the longest high-priority action list I have ever had. My co-workers teased me when I told them that I had put this list into an electronic spreadsheet and sorted it by the latest date that I could start each activity. But it worked!

The daily action list should include not only urgent activities, but important activities that are not urgent. It should also contain time set aside for your values. For example, if one of your values is physical fitness, you will want to include a related activity on your action list at least three times per week. If your priority values include spiritual growth, you will want to reflect this on your action list.

You might have a long paper to write for one of your classes. Since the paper is due at the end of the semester, it is important but not urgent at the beginning of the semester. You know that you will not be able to complete this paper in a day. It might require several days, weeks, or even months. In this case, you can divide this paper into manageable segments and develop milestones for the segments. This offers several benefits:

- The paper will not seem as overwhelming as it might have if you were to try to tackle it entirely at once.
- It is easier to concentrate on smaller tasks. The old saying that it is "easiest to eat an elephant one bite at a time" is true.
- By getting part of the paper done on a daily basis, you are in a better position to complete the paper on time and even have time to review and enhance it before it is due.
- You are working on something that you classify as important.

It is best to prioritize a daily action list at the beginning of the day or at the end of the preceding day. There are many ways to prioritize the daily list. One way would be to compare the tasks with your values and to give highest priorities to those items which correspond with your highest values.

Another way to prioritize your daily action list would be to use the ABC method, where you would assign an "A" to the imperative tasks, a "B" to the other important tasks, and a "C" to all other tasks. Once you have done this, take another look at the items to which you have assigned a "C" priority. Are these the things that you really need or want to do? This will be your decision. Once you have made this decision, you are ready to go ahead with your "A" priorities. When you have finished your "A" priorities, you are ready to start on your "B" priorities.

Many days, you will not complete all of the tasks on your action list. But, most days, you will complete your "A" priorities and some of your "B" priorities. You will then move the tasks, which have not been completed, to another day's list.

4. Make time for your highest priorities.

How often have you heard someone say, "I just do not have enough time"? The truth is that they have the exact same amount of time as you do, as I do, and as the successful college students and graduates in this book. The difference is in how they choose to spend or control their time and their tasks. To gain more control, it helps to ask ourselves, "Is this what I want or need to be doing right now?" If not, the prioritized action list will help to get back on track.

Learn to say no to requests and demands that do not fit into your priorities or help you to achieve your goals. In *101 Ways To Make Every Second Count*, Robert W. Bly says, "I had to learn to say no to requests, invitations, and offers that would neither make me happy nor help me to achieve my goals. But once I did it, I found that it was a liberating experience that gets easier with repetition."

Eliminate time-consuming activities that do not fit within your priority values. For me, scrubbing the kitchen floor every night was time-consuming. I value cleanliness, but this was carrying it to the extreme. I found that I could scrub the floor less often, and my kitchen was still clean enough. This freed some of my time to do the things that I enjoyed most and which contributed to my success.

One of my values is to give of myself to others. Many years ago, I took up the hobby of counted cross-stitching. I would spend hundreds of hours on one wall hanging and then give it to a friend or family member as a gift. A friend once asked how much time I had spent on a particular gift. She then calculated how much money this gift was worth by multiplying the number of hours by the hourly rate I would have made if I had been working at my occupation during the hours that I spent creating this gift. The amount was staggering; however, the gift was priceless to the receiver, I had engaged in an activity that I enjoyed, and the creation of this gift was within my value priorities. By freeing up my time in other ways, I was able to spend more time on this priority activity.

* * * * *

To create success in our lives, we need to define and prioritize our values and to live by the priorities we set for ourselves.

Mishana Hosseinioun, a third-year student at U.C. Berkeley, currently has a 3.9 grade point average. At age nineteen, she speaks, reads and writes six languages. Although she has not yet declared a major, she is planning a double major in Rhetoric and Near Eastern Studies. She said, "Throughout my life, my success has relied on my ability to spend my personal energy wisely, generously, and with confidence. The key lies in recognizing the appropriate time and place for exerting myself, and more precisely, in knowing *which* endeavors are worthy of my dear time and energy and will yield the best return in the long run. Such may involve being able to view educational lectures, artistic performances, and special evenings out with my parents as healthier, long-term weekend alternatives to, say, some impersonal and fruitless parties."

This is not to say that parties are not important. As you will see in chapter 9, taking time for recreation is also a strong contributor to success. We all choose different types of recreation, which helps us to refresh ourselves and to create balance in our lives. Mishana knows her priorities and lives them. This contributes significantly to her success.

As I interviewed people for this book, one of the most-mentioned priorities had to do with balance in life. Stephanie Kane, who graduated from the University of Dayton, Ohio, is a business planning associate at General Mills and an avid golfer. In college, she was a scholarship athlete and also had an academic scholarship. She worked two or three jobs at a time, while holding leadership positions in two clubs. Just as important to her, she maintained several critical friendships and relationships through college. She said, "I never sacrificed my personal life for my commitments. I managed my time so effectively that I was able to be successful at work, at school, and at sports. My relationships were my number one priority. If they weren't going well, nothing seemed like it was." Stephanie added that her most outstanding accomplishment has been her ability to balance so many responsibilities in her life.

When I talked with successful college students, they highlighted the following priorities:

- Excelling in school
- Close relationships
- Positive friendships
- Future career
- Physical fitness
- Being a good person
- Enjoying life
- Financial security in the future

The priorities of successful college graduates are similar:
- Balance in life
- Relationship with spouse and family
- Success in business or a career
- Fulfilling my purpose in life
- Serving God
- Spirituality
- Having a vision and goals
- Health and wellness
- Creating wealth
- Traveling and learning about other cultures
- Providing for safety, well-being, and happiness of family
- Having a successful family by setting an example of success in business, marriage, parenting, friendships,

and productivity
- Having a life that is abundant in joy
- Personal satisfaction

Nicholas Kahler, a graduate of the United States Military Academy (West Point), is now an Army artillery officer in the Third Armored Cavalry Regiment. He was in the top 20 percent of his class at West Point (no easy accomplishment), made good friends, and was passionate about being an Army leader. After his return from active duty in Iraq, he said, "I've learned within the last year that the ability to manage my own perspective is the trait that contributed most to my success or failure. My idea of managing perspective is the active evaluation and adaptation of your own thought process. Periodically taking time to step away from the here and now, and evaluating where your attention and priorities should be, is a learned skill that becomes simple over time. Introspection and evaluation will help you to determine if your 'lens' is zoomed too close or too wide. Fortunately, I've done this in some form or another, but only realized and named it in the last year."

Dr. Nathan Wood, who is now a licensed marriage and family therapist, said that, when he was an undergraduate, he defined success by the grade he received. "I knew I needed to get into grad school, and grades mattered," he said. During grad school, he measured his success more in terms of applying knowledge. Because he stuck to his priority list in college, he knew he was better prepared for success in his career. He stated, "At some point in college, probably in graduate school, learning and application became more important than the grade. That love of learning and curiosity is still one of my greatest assets in my career. If I follow my priority list, all of the other success strategies fall into place on their own."

By using the methods specified in this chapter, we are able to make time to do those things that are most important to us. When our values are prioritized before writing a "to do" list, we are better able to determine when an *urgent* item is an *important* item and act accordingly.

Chapter Four

Set Powerful Goals!

Maximize your achievement

My first quarter in college almost seemed like an academic disaster. Since I had excelled at a private high school, I had expected that college would be easy. I had been excited about going to college and about the independence it would give me. Although my dorm room did not compare to the luxury and comfort I had at home, I still thought it was the best. My roommate had a great personality, and we got along well. Putting the professors on a pedestal, I enjoyed all of my classes. Well, I enjoyed most of my classes, except geography. By the end of the first quarter, I was almost ready to give up.

I was lucky to end the first quarter with a 2.5 grade point average. Fortunately, my parents were quite lenient when they saw this, even though I had earned mostly A's in high school. I just knew I could do better the next quarter, and I did. I finished the second quarter with a 2.75 grade point average for the quarter.

Knowing that the third quarter would be the last before my wedding and that I might not be able to return to school for several years, I decided to make this quarter count. Although the classes were as challenging as the ones I took during the first two quarters,

I wrote myself a note that I would earn an A in every class that quarter. By the time the grades arrived, I was working full time. My mother called me at work, which she has seldom done in all the years that I have been working. You can probably imagine my excitement when I heard her say, "I couldn't wait until you came home tonight to tell you this. Your grade point average for the third quarter is 4.0." If we don't count the first two quarters, I've never had a grade point average under 3.7 since that time.

For me, the difference between the third quarter and the first two quarters was that I had a well-defined goal. I committed my goal to paper, and I did the things that I needed to do to achieve the goal.

My office dictionary defines the word *goal* as "the purpose toward which effort is directed." We are all engaged in some type of effort each day, but are we all working toward a known purpose? If you have read Lewis Carroll's *Through the Looking Glass*, you might remember the quote, "If you don't know where you're going, any road will get you there." To be successful, it is important to know where it is that you want to go.

Do you know where you are going? Do you know the purpose toward which your efforts are directed? Successful people set goals and direct their efforts toward achieving them. However, fewer than 5 percent of all people have goals. In the course of my career, I have heard the following excuses for not setting goals:

- *"I am a busy person. I don't have time to think about setting goals."* I hope this person reads chapter 3 of this book on determining values and setting priorities.
- *"It doesn't pay for me to set goals, because I keep changing my mind about what I want."* One of the steps in the goal-setting process is to clarify wants and needs.
- *"I set a goal once and didn't achieve it."* I question whether this person was committed to the goal and whether she had developed an action plan for achieving the goal. There will be more on this later.

The first step to achieving a goal is to *have* a goal. Jeff Notto, a graduate of St. Thomas University, has had goals longer than he can remember. When he was twelve years old, his dad owned an auto repair garage. Jeff's goal at that time was to learn about business from his dad, so he was excited when his dad asked him to work in the garage during the summer. His responsibilities at that time included cleaning parts and assisting the mechanics. "My favorite project was loading the pop machine," he said, "because, when I was finished, Dad would always let me have a nice cold Coke."

After learning about business from his dad, Jeff set a goal to start his own business when he was in high school. While working on the school newspaper and yearbook, he learned enough about photography to start a photography business when he was a junior in high school. He became a sought-after wedding photographer and was booked almost every weekend during his senior year. By setting his business goal at such a young age, Jeff was able to learn some important business skills, including time management, customer relationship management, and the financial impact of owning a business. His photography business paid most of his college expenses and also enabled him to buy a car.

Because of his photography experience, Jeff was a member of the college yearbook staff and the photo editor for the college newspaper. Majoring in journalism with a minor in psychology, his next goal was to pursue a career in communications. While he was a junior in college, 3M offered him a position in its photography department. In this position, he was able to set his own hours, and, upon his graduation from college, 3M offered him a communications position.

As a college graduate and full-time employee, Jeff set some higher-level career goals, along with milestones to reach these goals. He has gone from communications to marketing to international business management. His time at 3M has included five-and-one-half years in Brussels, Belgium, where he coordinated the European business for two of 3M's divisions. Currently, he is responsible for the international business of one of 3M's business units. He travels extensively to Europe, Asia, Latin America, and Canada to work with 3M management in these areas in setting and achieving their business development goals.

In addition to being successful in business, Jeff is also successful in life. He says that his most significant accomplishment has been to marry his wife, Carol. Together, they have set a goal to be active in marriage ministry, and they have been an inspiration to countless married couples because of their work in this area.

Jeff said, "Setting your goals gives you the basis for a plan for achieving those goals. Early in my career, I knew I wanted to travel and to live in a different country. At that time, I didn't have a specific goal as to where I would travel or that I would live in a foreign country, but I let my desires help form my goals. Once my goals became clearer, I was able to accomplish them."

Wendy Richards is another goal-oriented college graduate. When she was very young, Wendy had a goal to live overseas. She thought about this goal while she was in high school and, when the time came, chose to attend a university that offered the possibility of an overseas experience. She decided that she wanted to live in Germany and began to study the German language, as well as the languages of neighboring countries. She met this goal and studied for a year in Berlin, while living with a German family.

After her year in Germany, Wendy returned to the United States and vigorously enhanced her goal to include working in Europe during her career. She graduated with a bachelor of arts degree in history at Stanford University, along with Phi Beta Kappa honors. She then continued on to Stanford's MBA program and graduated as the Arjay Miller Scholar. She was in the top 10 percent of her class.

Wendy's education prepared her well for international employment. After finishing her MBA, her first position was as an International Market Development Manager for Activision, where she established and managed European subsidiaries in England, France, and Germany and structured licensing agreements for Japan. By age thirty, she had become the director of International Strategic Planning for a large telecommunications company. She was later transferred to Brussels, Belgium, to serve as the managing director for that company in Belgium. Her career has progressed from that point to include top management positions in large international companies, where she has had the opportunity to live and work in several European countries.

Wendy started setting goals before college and continued doing so throughout college and afterward. She has accomplished every goal that she has set for herself. Not all of us start this process as young as she was, and many of us have taken gigantic detours along the way. This is especially true of me. However, I have learned the value of setting powerful goals and have been able to achieve phenomenal success as a result. It's never too late to start setting goals. You can start today and know that you will become even more successful than you are now.

Before setting goals, it is important to become extremely clear in determining what it is that we really want. In chapter 2, we discussed the visualization process, and you did some work in determining your wants and desires. Now that you have completed chapter 3 and determined your values and related priorities, it is time to revisit your list of choices from the visualization process. Are these choices congruent with your values and priorities in life? If not, now is the time to make some adjustments.

When I first determined that I wanted to live and work in Europe, I wasn't totally clear on where I wanted to live on the European continent. During my first visualization exercise, I pictured myself living in Brussels, Belgium. I later realized that this was because Brussels was the location of my company's European headquarters, and I thought that I had to live in Brussels in order to do the type of work that I wanted to do. Initially, I allowed my beliefs to limit my vision. As I clarified my goal, I realized that I really wanted to live near Paris, France, and still have the opportunity to spend as much of my business time as possible in Brussels. The clarification gave me the best of both worlds—a home in France and offices in both France and Belgium.

I truly believe that each of us is the CEO of our own life. In order for a person to be successful as a CEO, he needs to take charge of his life. He needs to realize that he creates the life he wants. Before doing this, he needs to know who he is and what he wants. He needs to seek clarity in doing this and in setting goals for his life.

In Bobbie Stevens' course and also in her book, *Unlimited Futures: How to Understand the Life You Have and Create the Life You Want*, she teaches what she calls "Seven Steps of the Creative Process." Visualization is one of these steps. Seeking clarity is another one. At one time in her life, Bobbie was very clear that she wanted to buy a townhouse, even though townhouses did not exist where she lived and she did not earn enough money at the time. With her clear goal and vision, however, she was able to create the steps necessary to accomplish this. She lists seeking clarity as the first step in creating what one wants in life.

Those who recognize the value of setting powerful goals are the people who create success. Many of these people are now enjoying success they would not have imagined had they not taken the time to set these goals. Goal setting is simple, once you have clarified your wants and desires. The following tips will help you to set and achieve powerful goals for yourself.

1. Write them down.

I once listened to a tape series where the speaker encouraged listeners to write on a piece of paper the amount of money they wanted to be making a year from then. He then said to seal the paper in an envelope and to wait one year to open the envelope. I wanted to be making much more money than I was earning at the time, but I worked for a corporation that had a set salary scale and ranges of percentages for salary increases. Nevertheless, I wrote down a number that was $30,000 more than I thought possible if I continued to work for this company. Although I did not change companies, I was thrilled one year later when I opened the envelope and discovered that my new salary was exactly what I had written. The contributing factors were that I had a goal, this goal was written, and I changed my work patterns to accomplish it. I also believe that, once a goal is written or "put out into the Universe" in another way, there are other factors that work with us in accomplishing this goal. For example, during this time, salary scales were changed, I received two promotions, and profit sharing for my company was at an all-time high. I had not considered these factors when I decided how much money I would like to be earning.

As I did, you might use this technique at the beginning of a semester to set a goal for the grades you will earn in all of your classes. Once you write this goal on paper or enter it into your computer, you will be better able to determine the action steps you need in order to accomplish this goal.

Less than 5 percent of all people have goals, and 3 percent have written goals. Since those with written goals are the ones who most often achieve their goals, they have difficulty understanding why the other 97 percent fail to write down their goals.

A goal becomes much more powerful when it is written down. Alexander Graham Bell observed, "What this power is I cannot say; all I know is that it exists, and it becomes available only when a man is in the state of mind in which he knows exactly what he wants and is fully determined not to quit until he finds it."

2. Ensure that your goals are realistic and achievable, but give them some "stretch" to allow room for growth.

My goal to earn all A's certainly had stretch, as did my goal to increase my income by an additional $30,000 per year. This is important in goal setting. Most of us don't realize the power within us to achieve greatness. The French spiritual philosopher, Teilhard de Chardin, said, "It is our duty to proceed as if limits to our ability do not exist." Successful people consistently set higher goals.

Are your goals big enough? Are they worthy of you? You were born with unlimited capacity in many areas. In these areas, you are limited only by your own thoughts and beliefs.

Terri Bowersock was born with dyslexia, a learning disability. She struggled through school and vividly recalls that one of her teachers hit her on the head with a ruler and exclaimed she was "as dumb as a cue ball." Terri herself could easily have believed she was stupid and incapable of accomplishing anything of value. She also could have believed that she would not be able to achieve any goals if she were to set them for herself; however, she was determined to succeed. She was able to graduate from high school, even though she could read only at a third-grade level. In her early twenties, she set a goal to become successful in the furniture consignment business, which was a business that hardly existed at that time. She started by borrowing $2,000 from her grandmother and opened a shop. Her first sales were her mother's living room furniture and her own bedroom set. She progressed from there, setting and achieving powerful goals along the way. She now owns and manages five companies, has more than twenty consignment furniture stores nationwide, and continues to expand her enterprises. Her annual sales exceed $30 million, and she is a sought-after motivational speaker. She has been named "Entrepreneurial Woman of the Year" by *Entrepreneur Magazine* and has won the *Inc.* magazine "Retail Entrepreneur of the Year" award. When she was featured on the *Oprah Winfrey Show*, Oprah said, "Terri knows the secrets to realize her dreams." This all started when Terri set her first goal to open a furniture consignment store.

You can use Terri's goal-setting techniques while you are in college. The keys are to know what you want to accomplish and to think big.

Many of us have physical limitations that must be taken into consideration when we set our goals. However, in case after case, I have seen people circumvent these physical limitations and set and achieve goals that strengthen them. Some may need to think about setting powerful goals in alternate areas of their lives where they are not affected by the physical limitation. Regardless, we can all set powerful goals and achieve them.

3. Clearly define your goals.

As you write a goal, it is important to give a clear definition of the results you want. Check to ensure that it answers the following "W" questions:

- Who? (In most cases, this will be you.)
- What? (We need to describe the end result of our goal.)
- Where? (This has to do with location. If it is an academic goal, it might be your college or university.)
- When? (Include the date on which the goal will be accomplished. If it is a long-term goal, it is also good to include some milestone dates.)

Once you are sure that the goal answers the "W" questions, check the goal to make sure that it is measurable. Ask yourself, "How will I know that I have achieved this goal?"

Becky Creighton says that one of the things that has most helped her to be successful is a clear understanding of her goals and what she is willing to do to achieve them. She asks herself the following questions:

- Is it important to me?
- Am I satisfied?
- Will it make my life turn out the way I want it to?

She says, "It sounds simple, but it is powerful in the sense that I don't get caught up in things that don't matter."

K. D. Taylor has also clearly defined her goals, both while she was in college and since then as a teacher and associate dean. She said, "By setting goals, I have given myself direction and motivation. If a person has no goals, (s)he is not likely to feel any pressure to move forward. We push ourselves along by the goals we set. When we have a clear picture of what we want to achieve, we can move in that direction to make it happen. By knowing I wanted to be a good teacher, I made certain that I was constantly moving in that direction."

* * * * *

Born in rural Arkansas, Kathy Brittain White was the daughter of a construction worker and a high school home economics teacher. She didn't think much about goals when she graduated from high school, but she thought that she wanted to finish college and follow in her mother's footsteps as a home economics teacher. As an eighteen-year-old college freshman, she married a serviceman who was transferred from base to base. She would go with him and take some college courses wherever they were living. Since she had taken secretarial courses, she was secure in the thought that she could always find a good office job wherever they lived. When she and her husband returned to Arkansas, she was pregnant with her second child. "We were broke and living in a horrible place," she told me. One day, she said she experienced a defining moment. "This is the way it is always going to be if I don't make it different," she realized. She then set a powerful educational goal for herself. She started university correspondence courses during her pregnancy and completed her undergraduate degree in a year. "I kept going to school," she said. "I just went on. I got a graduate assistantship at the University of Arkansas. I never stopped until I finished my doctorate."

Kathy's goals became even more powerful. The year that she completed her doctorate degree, she became an associate professor at the University of North Carolina, conducting primary and secondary research on information technology best practices, systems implementation success, and metrics. She wrote more than thirty articles that were published in major publications and spoke frequently in her area of expertise at national and international conferences.

Kathy continued on her goal-oriented path. Her next goal was to become an executive in the corporate world. She moved from the education world into the corporate world as the vice president of a major corporation. When I interviewed her, she was the executive vice president and chief information officer of a major healthcare company. At that time, her worldwide staff totaled more than 1,500 people. She continues to clearly define her goals, which include family, relationships, career, and making a significant contribution in the world.

4. Visualize your goals as if you have already achieved them.

How do you feel about your goals? Do they excite you? Do they provide emotional energy? Do you dream about them at night? Do they get you up in the morning with a feeling of vigor for doing what needs to be done in order to achieve them? If not, you need to reevaluate your goals, values, and priorities.

For most of you, the time you are in college is an exciting time of your life. Even if it is not, you might look at it as a means to reach an exciting future goal.

Once you have clearly defined goals that excite you and to which you are committed, revisit chapter 2 and repeat the visualization process for these goals. You originally engaged in this process to visualize what you thought you wanted the first time you read chapter 2. Now you can become even more clear in your visualization. Henry David Thoreau stated it quite succinctly when he said, "If you have built castles in the air, your work need not be lost; that is where they should be. Now put the foundations under them." You can do this by setting, being committed to, continuing to visualize, and taking action on your goals.

For many students, concrete images of the results of these goals are also helpful. You might want to cut pictures from magazines or catalogues that will remind you of your goals. For example, if your goal is to have your own apartment, you can find or draw a picture of the floor plan of this apartment and put it in a place where you will see it often (your refrigerator, your bathroom mirror, etc.). One student, who wanted to get down to her high school graduation dress size, taped a picture of herself at this size to her refrigerator. A student who wants to study in Paris might do the same with pictures of the Eiffel Tower, *Notre Dame* Cathedral, and the *Arc de Triomphe*. These concrete, easily recognizable pictures will help you in the visualization process.

Goal setting significantly increases our opportunity for success. It is my belief that combining visualization with goal setting exponentially increases the successful outcome. In *The Law of Success*, Napoleon Hill said, "Any definite chief aim that is deliberately fixed in the mind and held there, with the determination to realize it, finally saturates the entire subconscious mind until it automatically influences the physical action of the body toward the attainment of that purpose."

I recommend that you visualize your goals by using the process in chapter 2 at least twice a day. The results that can be achieved by running these mental movies are much, much greater than the amount of time it takes to do this. You are capable of greatness. Visualization will give the information to the subconscious mind, enabling it to help you in achieving your highest aspirations.

The Eastern sage and philosopher, Patanjali, once said, "When you are inspired by some great purpose, some extraordinary project, all your thoughts break their bounds. Your mind transcends limitations, your consciousness expands in every direction . . . Dominant forces, faculties and talents become alive, and you discover yourself to be a greater person by far than you ever dreamed yourself to be."

5. Describe the benefits of your goals.

According to Dr. Dennis Deaton, a goal becomes more powerful when its benefits are expressed in the form of two specific statements:

- Personal, or self-directed, benefits
- Altruistic, or spiritual, benefits

Dr. Deaton recommends the development of a "Power Goal Manuscript," which includes the statement of the goal (including who, what, where, and when), a benefit statement, and a commitment statement.

When I first wrote my goal for living and working in Europe, I included the following benefit statement, which you read in chapter 2:

I am excited about this excellent opportunity to not only increase the company's sales and marketing effectiveness in Europe and enhance my career, but also to see and experience much of Europe, including the Vatican and the Leaning Tower of Pisa in Italy, the Eiffel Tower and the Louvre in Paris, the theater in London, the green rolling landscape of Ireland, the Alps, ancient cathedrals and museums.

My husband Cliff and I look forward to making new acquaintances with many Europeans whom we will meet in the next two years. We are also eager to host many of our American friends and relatives in Europe.

I later added the following to this benefit statement:

As we look at the house, I think about how this will be my home base as I travel to seventeen different countries in Europe in developing a sales and marketing productivity plan. What an opportunity this is to contribute to the company's growth! By increasing sales and marketing productivity in Europe, 3M's sales in Europe will grow by at least 5 percent. I am excited about the opportunity to contribute to driving this growth.

I am also looking forward to being active in my church in Europe, to being a leader in the church's women's organization, and to touching the hearts of many women through its education program.

Reviewing these benefits daily helped me to visualize and achieve my goal. Your benefit statement can be a paragraph or a list. Whichever you choose, you'll want to make sure you can picture the benefits you describe. The pictures will then translate best to your subconscious mind as you engage in the visualization process.

6. Commit to accomplishing your goals.

When I wrote my goal for living and working in Europe, I included the following commitment statement:

> *I commit myself totally to this goal. I commit myself to continuing to learn about productivity through books, magazines, videotapes, audiotapes, and seminars. I see myself working with others who specialize in this field. I see Cliff and I working together to prepare for this move.*
>
> *I commit myself to networking with those in the company who can assist in making this happen. This will include area vice presidents, managing directors, and human resource personnel.*
>
> *I commit myself to developing a plan for building a sales and marketing productivity architecture for Europe. I will put my best effort into developing and implementing this plan.*

If we are not willing to do what is needed in order to accomplish a goal, we may as well not even have a goal. A person might say that their goal is to be a millionaire. When asked what they are going to do to become a millionaire, they have no answer. Their goal is not a goal at all, but a fantasy. Goals require commitment and action.

This is the same for a student whose goal is a 4.0 grade point average. The student needs to commit to accomplishing this goal. Without commitment, there is very little chance that it will happen.

7. Develop and implement an action plan.

As you engage in the visualization process, you picture yourself as if you have already achieved your goal. Your subconscious mind will help you to develop the process to get there, if you are in tune with and listen to its promptings. Some people call these promptings "intuition." As you receive these promptings, pay attention to them. Then write them down.

Even early American leaders took intuitive thoughts seriously. Thomas Paine once said, "Any person who has made observations on the state of progress of the human mind cannot but have observed that there are two distinct classes of what are called thoughts: Those that we produce by ourselves by reflection and the act of thinking, and those that bolt into the mind on their own accord. I have always made it a rule to treat these voluntary visitors with civility, taking care to examine, as well as I was able, if they were worth entertaining; and it is from them I have acquired almost all the knowledge I have."

Italian artist Leonardo da Vinci stated, "The ideas that would suddenly come to my awareness proved to be most worthy and were in the end found to be infallible in leading me to discoveries of great importance."

These thoughts that bolt into our minds are often golden in nature. They have the potential to both solve problems and open doors of opportunity. They usually come during our most quiet times, as those are the times that we are most open to listening to them. I often receive these inspirational messages in the shower, as I am relaxing under the hot water. Others will receive these messages in the middle of the night during one of their lighter sleep cycles. It is advisable to have a tape recorder or paper and pen nearby in order to record these messages. These thoughts can also come during or immediately following a visualization session, prayer, or meditation. During these times, you may want to remain in your position for a few moments in order to receive these messages, and then write them down. Revisit your notes soon afterward to sort them out in your mind while they are still fresh.

As you start to develop your action plan for a major goal, you might want to engage in a brainstorming process with yourself. Start by writing your goal at the top of a piece of paper. During the next twenty minutes, write at least twenty things that you can do to accomplish this goal. As you are writing, do not ponder whether these things are possible; just keep writing. When you think you have thought of everything you can do to accomplish the goal, write five more things. The first five things you write will be obvious and probably will be things that anyone would have written. The more you write, the more your subconscious mind will deliver. The best ideas often will come after you have written sixteen or seventeen items.

You are now ready to develop your action plan for accomplishing your goal. If your goal is a long-term one, it will work best to divide it into shorter-term action plans. For example, if your goal involves writing a paper for a twelve-week class, you might develop action plans for each week. If you are writing a thesis or dissertation for an advanced degree, it might be more appropriate to write three-month action plans. After each three-month period, you can then evaluate and make adjustments in the plans for future segments. On the surface, large goals can seem intimidating. However, even ninety-day goals can be divided into a series of smaller action steps that are easy to plan, easy to integrate into daily activities, and fairly easy to accomplish. By doing this, you can accomplish even long-term, strategic goals without becoming overwhelmed.

In addition to listing the steps you will take to accomplish your goal, you will want to include the following in your plan:

- Resources needed
- Possible obstacles and alternative ways to work around these obstacles
- Support structure currently in place
- Type of support you will need in order to accomplish the goal
- Interim rewards for accomplishing action steps
- How you will measure your goals

Keith Geilman, a graduate of Utah State University and successful sales manager, said, "I am a work in process. I am a human becoming, not a human being. I am still working on goals that are important to me. The goals must also be consistent with the principles of my personal philosophy. To achieve said goals, it is my belief that those goals must be defined in such a manner that they can be measured. Once the goals have been defined, then a support team needs to be assembled, told about the goals, and then asked to be coaches."

Brian Tracy, a popular motivational speaker, gives the following tips for goal achievement:

- Identify your major obstacles to goal achievement. Ask yourself what stands between you and your goal. Some examples could be a relationship, health concerns, education, your boss, etc.
- Set a deadline and a schedule for accomplishment.
- Set a schedule for rewarding yourself as you reach milestones on the way to accomplishing your goal.
- Review your goals every morning and every evening.
- Be clear about what you want to accomplish.

He also recommends that you keep your mind on your previous successes.

As you have been reading this chapter, I hope you have taken the time to write your major goals and ensure that they are aligned with your values and priorities in life. If you do not have written goals, I encourage you to write them now. If you want to create success in your life, this will be well worth the investment in time.

Dream big, and set powerful goals around these dreams. Ask yourself what goal you would set for yourself if you knew you would successfully achieve it. Next, ask yourself if this is what you really want. If it is, write it down. Then you can use what you have learned in this chapter to put yourself on the path to achieving this goal. A speaker at a conference I attended recently said, "Goals are the fuel in the furnace of achievement." By setting powerful goals, you can maximize your achievement.

Chapter Five

Ready—Aim—Take Action!

Start NOW!

Abraham Lincoln said, "Things may come to those who wait, but only the things left by those who hustle." We build a foundation by visualizing what we want, determining our priorities, and setting goals. Once this is done, it is necessary to move forward by *taking action*. Standing still is the fastest way of moving backwards in this rapidly changing world.

As you engage in the visualization process, your subconscious mind will help you to develop an action plan to meet your goals. Sigmund Freud once declared, "Thought is action in rehearsal." Many successful athletes, as well as business people, put this concept into practice. One example is Jack Nicklaus, one of the most successful professional golfers, who said, "I never hit a shot, not even in practice, without having a very sharp, in-focus picture of it in my head. It's like a color movie. First I 'see' the ball where I want it to finish, nice and white sitting up high on the bright green grass. Then the scene quickly changes, and I 'see' the ball going there: its path, trajectory and shape, even its behavior on the landing. Then there is a fade-out, and the next scene shows me making the kind of swing that will turn the previous images into reality."

Jack Nicklaus uses visualization to create his success; however, he doesn't stop there. Immediately after visualizing the success, he takes action to ensure this success. Taking action differentiates those who only dream from those who have dreams and create success in their lives.

In physical stature, Charleen Tajiri is one of the most petite women I have ever met. When she first entered our meeting, I wondered to myself if she buys her clothes in the children's department!Within minutes after she began her presentation, I had forgotten about her physical size. I was much more impressed with her dynamism, professionalism, and confidence. She is a successful businesswoman, who knows where she's headed and acts quickly to achieve her goals.

The first of six children, Charleen was raised by a single mother in a home with few, if any luxuries. She attended the University of Hawaii, the only one in her family to go to college. But, it wasn't until she was thirty years old that she started to take charge of her life. Almost immediately, she became successful.

She did some volunteer work at a personal growth and development company. The company hired her as an employee a year later. She rose to the top of the company by working hard and developing strong management and leadership skills. Although her home was, and still is, in Honolulu, her reputation as a leader spread across the United States. As a result, a much larger seminar company on the mainland approached her and asked her to work for them from her Hawaii home office. She accepted the position and, within the first year, doubled the attendance at this company's seminars.

While holding leadership positions in the development and seminar companies, Charleen was also involved as a distributor for multiple companies, which sold their products through multilevel marketing channels. She quickly became a top distributor for each one of these companies. She is currently an executive director with a company that rewards its people according to their results, and Charleen knows that well-thought-out action produces results.

Charleen believes in running a principle-centered business. Her family is her top priority. Her office is in her home, and this helps her to spend more time with her son. Her home is always open to family and friends. She is results-driven and takes the appropriate action to achieve successful results. She says, "It's when I take action that things really happen, even those things that I may not have thought about during the planning stage. More options and solutions seem to pop up as I'm working to achieve a goal."

Charleen agrees with Thomas Edison's statement, "Genius is 1 percent inspiration and 99 percent perspiration." For her, the inspiration is the necessary foundation, but the action actually accomplishes the goal. Other successful graduates in this book agree:

Becky Creighton, successful real estate investor and Ohio State University graduate, says, "Taking action seems so apparent as to its importance to being successful. I can talk all I want about what I want to do and the goals I want to achieve, but, if I don't put my body in action, my goals won't be achieved."

Keith Geilman, successful sales manager and Utah State University graduate, says, "Daily action with focus toward a goal will result with greater success than is imaginable to most people. It is unfortunate that I have to keep remembering this principle, and I did not fully understand the implications of action until later in my life and, as a result, I may not have achieved the full extent of success that was before me."

Nicholas Kahler, successful Army artillery officer and West Point Military Academy graduate, says, "The world moves quickly, and if you're not prepared, you'll be left behind. People in all fields are hired to make decisions and move on things. I've always used my own knowledge and that of those around me to make important decisions (and take action). This helps a lot in the town of Fallujah, Iraq."

Rebecca O'Neill, successful attorney and University of Florida graduate, says, "One cannot sit and wait for opportunity to fall into one's lap. If some form of action needs to be taken, and I volunteer or jump in and perform, that action gets noticed by all, not just by the bosses, but also by the judges, clients, and co-workers, and it sets a good example."

Stephanie Kane, successful business planning associate and University of Dayton, Ohio graduate, says, "Taking action is number one. I can talk all I want about the things I want in life, but if I don't physically do anything about it, it's only that—just talk. By networking, going to career fairs, moving to Arizona, practicing golf, going places to meet people, and visiting new countries or cities every year, I am taking action, even if it's just baby steps, toward my larger goals."

* * * * *

Jim Paschal achieved a 4.0 grade point average at Arizona State University and graduated number one in his class. He says he achieved this primarily because of good study habits and because of relentless perseverance to the pursuit of his goals.

Jim said, "Some of the most important success traits that I acquired while I was in college were self-discipline, ability to multitask, and the ability to organize. Studying materials in college and completing homework is a challenge any student can relate to and is necessary to achieve good grades. What may not be obvious is that the good habits I developed in this regard paved the way for future career and life advancements. What is also significant about this is that, before college, I was not at all disciplined and rarely ever completed goals."

A lesson from Jim is that good habits can be formed at any time, and the best time is now. Even if you have not formed good study habits before now, you can do it starting now by taking action to do so.

Jim is action-oriented as well as goal oriented. He has been successful in his career and is currently pursuing his childhood dream to develop and market the world's first flying car, a vehicle that anyone can learn to fly. Still in the early stages of the project, he is creating a corporation to redesign his last aircraft prototype and take the project forward. He says, "Knowledge is worthless unless you are willing to use it to see your desired goals come to fruition in your career or in your personal life." An example of this is how Jim fulfilled his lifelong dream of flying his own aircraft. Over a grueling period of eight years and many long hours, he designed and built his aircraft. He finally realized his goal when he actually flew it. He adds, "The key to remember is that the reason I accomplished this, when at least 100 other flyboys that I met over the years all failed in their attempts to get their machines airborne, is that I never gave up." He kept taking action until he succeeded.

When Jim worked for a larger company, his reputation was that he was "the guy to go to because he gets things done." Taking action, along with his ability to set goals, prioritize what is important, and believing that he will achieve his goals contributed to his reputation then and continues to contribute to his success in his career and in his life.

* * * * *

All of the successful students, who interviewed for this book, agreed that action is a predecessor to success. One student said, "Just do it!" Another said, "If you don't act, nothing will happen." A graduate quoted Will Rogers, who stated, "Even if you're on the right track, you'll get run over if you just sit there."

Often the most difficult part of taking action is getting started. The best way to start is to first develop an action plan. Writing an action plan requires an action itself—that of writing. Your action plan can be simple or complex, depending on the nature of your goal. Following are examples of some simple action plans:

1. My worst grade in college was in geography, a required course in which I had very little interest. Now that I have traveled the world and worked in several different countries, I wish I would have paid more attention in my geography class so many years ago. I'm sure that, if I had set a goal and developed an action

plan for learning geography, I would have learned more and earned a better grade for the course. My action plan might have contained the following items:

- Arrive at geography class at least five minutes early each day, and be prepared to listen and take notes as soon as the class starts.
- Take excellent notes during class.
- If my mind starts wandering during class, force myself to bring it back to class.
- Read at least eight pages of the geography textbook each day, and highlight the most important information.
- Each week, engage in additional research on the places we are studying. (When I went to school, this research would have been done at the library. Now it can be done on the Internet.)
- Look for information in the lessons, in the text, and in my outside research that most interests me.
- Visualize the places we are studying.
- Review my notes at the end of each week.
- Spend at least as much time studying geography as I spend studying for the classes I enjoy.
- Study diligently for exams.
- Reward myself for following this action plan.

2. Jennifer, who is a college senior, has a goal to decrease the size of clothing she wears from a 14 to a 10. Her action plan might include these steps:

- Visualize myself as wearing a size 10.
- Tape pictures to the refrigerator and bathroom mirror of myself from three years ago, when I wore a size 10.
- Consult with my doctor concerning the diet that is best for me.
- When eating in the cafeteria, look for low-fat, low-carbohydrate, and low-calorie foods that provide the nutrition I need.
- Prepare weekly menu plans for eating at home.
- Make grocery lists before shopping for groceries.
- Shop for groceries after meals, and buy only those foods on the list.

- Eat only foods that are on my diet plan.
- Walk or run at least thirty minutes each day.
- Weigh and measure myself weekly.
- Reward myself by attending a concert or going to a movie as I reach each five-pound milestone.

3. Adam is a college freshman, and his goal is learn more about a foreign culture by traveling to France during the summer after his sophomore year. He will develop a long-term action plan containing the following items, and this plan will serve as a basis for developing more-detailed short-term plans.

   - Develop learning and recreational objectives for the trip.
   - Do some research on France on the Internet, and read some related books and magazine articles.
   - Make a list of the cities I will visit and the specific sites I will see, as well as the things I will do.
   - Visualize the sites I will see in France, and keep a notebook with clippings of these sites.
   - Research lodging and transportation alternatives, including associated costs.
   - Prepare a preliminary budget for the trip.
   - Determine how I will finance the trip. (This will lead to additional action plans.)
   - Continue taking classes in French to increase my proficiency in the language.

4. Before you started college, you probably had set a goal to complete your bachelor's degree. Since this also is a longer-term goal, it requires some decision analysis, as well as short-term action steps. If you had written your action plan, some of the steps in the plan would have been similar to the following:

   - Visualize myself at a college commencement walking to the stage in cap and gown to receive my diploma.
   - Determine the major area of study that best fits what I want to do in the future.
   - Determine how I will finance my education.
   - Decide on whether to go to a local college or to move to another city.
   - Make a list of things that are most important to me

regarding my education as well as programs offered by a college.

- Research colleges and universities that offer a program in my major area of study. This research can be conducted through visits to my local library, through a search on the Internet, and by talking with college students and recent graduates.
- Select the colleges that best meet my criteria.
- Send applications to these colleges.

You might also have had a concurrent action plan describing the preparations you needed to make in order to make this goal a priority. This will include a plan for making the time available to study and a plan describing how you will handle your other top priorities, such as work and/or family. You might also have had a long-term action plan in place with some broadly defined steps to help you to meet your goal of earning your bachelor's degree within a specific time period.

5. Heather is completing her degree in business management and will be interviewing for a position with a large company next week. She is excited about this interview and has prepared the following action plan:

    - Each day, visualize myself walking into the interview and answering the questions with self-confidence.
    - Learn as much as I can about the company by reviewing its Web site and reading its annual report.
    - Think about the types of questions that the interviewer might ask, and determine how I would answer them.
    - Make a list of questions I will ask the interviewer about the company.
    - Think about the benefits I might be able to offer this employer.
    - Prepare a folder with information about myself that might interest the interviewer.
    - Ask my friend, Christy, if she will role play the interview with me and give me constructive feedback on how I can improve. (Of course, I'll do the same for her when she starts interviewing for potential jobs.)

- Determine what I will wear for the interview to ensure that I look professional.
- After the interview, follow up with a thank-you letter to the interviewer.

Once you have developed your action plan, you can include the appropriate steps in your prioritized daily action plans. This will help you to ensure that you are working on your high-priority goals each day.

* * * * *

Marilyn Straka, a graduate of Macalester College in St. Paul, Minnesota, has enjoyed much success in her Information Technology career. A shy high school student, she decided to overcome her shyness when she went to college. She said she took small steps to become more outgoing and realized that was much more fun. She gained self-confidence and emerged from her small world into a much larger one by becoming proactive in meeting and developing friendships with people from a variety of backgrounds.

Marilyn's childhood dream was to work with the disabled. While she had planned to pursue her goal after college, her circumstances led her to accepting a computer programming position. Although she excelled in the Information Technology field and was successful following this career path, she never forgot her dream. She constantly sought volunteer work and ways of helping people.

Living in hilly San Francisco, Marilyn saw her dream taking shape when she began to plan her second career, a business to take seniors and disabled people on adventures to parks and outdoor destinations where they normally couldn't go. At first, she thought this would happen when she retired after her son finished college. However, a friend, a breast cancer survivor who knows the value of each day, encouraged her to follow her dream NOW. She began taking action by revising her business plan and outlined walks that could be done by the disabled on their own. This meant they were on level ground—no hills or steps! She documented the points of interest and made notes where further research was needed.

With the experience Marilyn had gained in business, along with her vision, goal, and action plan, she founded her own business, which she calls "On The Level." She offers walking tours for disabled persons and seniors, and has written and published several tour books on the same subject.

Marilyn says, "When people don't do what they are asked, the reason may be that they don't know how to get started. Break any large task into small measurable pieces. Then DO IT. Make that first phone call, give that first speech, clean the first room, and move forward. The first time I make a call to a new market, I may not know the business or terminology, so I ask a lot of questions. Then the second call goes more smoothly. The key here is to take action. Many people have good ideas or good intentions, but the task seems overwhelming. Take that first small step, and the others will follow."

What are your action steps for achieving your goals? If you have not yet written them, do it now. When you develop your action plan, you will want to consider how suitable it is to you and your situation, the amount of time required to complete each step, any outside forces or influences that might affect the plan, and your commitment to the plan.

As you are taking action, you are making decisions. Everything you do in life requires decisions. You make a decision to get out of bed in the morning. You decide what to wear, whether you should put gas in your car now or wait until it is almost empty (if you have a car), whether to make a phone call, what to buy when you are shopping, and what to eat for dinner tonight. When there may be several alternative actions for a situation or if the action will have a major impact on your life, you might want to engage in a decision analysis. In one of the sample action plans described earlier, you might have engaged in a decision analysis to determine which college best met all of your criteria.

After having been a Minnesota state systems analyst for four years, I engaged in a decision analysis after setting a goal to learn more about business by working as a systems analyst in a nongovernment organization. My goal was to find a new position within the next month. I had three prerequisites for this position:

- The salary for this position must be at least as much as my current salary.
- The position must be in an IBM mainframe environment, where COBOL was the major programming language used. (This was a long time ago!)
- The location where I would work must be within driving distance of my current home.

I started by responding to local newspaper ads and contacting a local information systems search firm. My efforts resulted in interviews at four companies and job offers from all four of them within a week. All four met my three prerequisites. I asked the human resource manager at each company for one week to think about the offer before responding. They all agreed. During this time, I performed a decision analysis using the following process, which will also work for you when you are choosing from among several alternatives.

Step I:

On a piece of paper, draw a chart showing the alternative decisions (in this case, the four job offers) across the top and the decision-making criteria along the left side. Under each alternative, leave room for two columns that will be used later in this analysis.

I listed the four companies along the top. On the left side, I listed criteria such as initial salary, benefits package, types of projects that would be assigned to me, opportunity for advancement, college tuition reimbursement program, working environment, my comfort level with the interviewer, reputation of the company, driving distance from my home, cost of parking, etc.

Step 2:

For each criterion, assign a weight between 1 and 5, and write this weight next to the criterion.

> *I gave salary a weight of "2," since my prerequisite was that the salary had to be at least equal to my current salary. All offers were more than my current salary, and they were all within 4 percent of each other. A larger weight would have skewed this to be more important than it was to me at the time. I went on to weight the benefits package a "4," types of projects a "5," etc.*

Step 3:

Evaluate each alternative for each criterion by assigning a score between 0 and 5, with "5" meaning the alternative very highly meets the criterion and "0" meaning that the alternative does not at all meet the criterion. Write the score in the cell (the box at the cross-section of the alternative and the criterion).

> *When I went through this step, I gave the first company a "3," the second company a "4," the third company a "4," and the fourth company a "3" for initial salary. The first company had an excellent benefits package, and I gave it a "5" in this area. I gave a score of "4" to each of the other companies for benefits. I then went on to score each of the criteria for each of the companies.*

Step 4:

Multiply the weight of the criterion by the score of the criterion for each alternative. Write this number in a separate column under each alternative.

> *I made sure that I had two columns under each company, one for the score and the other for the score multiplied by the weight. I performed the calculations and entered them on my chart.*

Step 5:

Add the weighted scores for each alternative.

*I performed this calculation, which gave me
one total for each company.*

Step 6:

Compare the totals. (If one of the totals is significantly higher than the others, this is the alternative that best meets the criteria. If there is not a significant difference between the highest total and the second highest total, you can either make a judgment call or add more criteria.)

This type of decision analysis can now be aided by the use of a computer spreadsheet.

From my decision analysis, I was able to determine that the offer from 3M was the one that best fit my criteria.

* * * * *

I stayed with the company for more than twenty-six years, had opportunities to develop and to make significant contributions, and was promoted throughout the ranks to be in the top 1 percent of the more than 75,000 employees. These facts demonstrated to me that it was well worth the time I took many years ago to perform a simple decision analysis to determine which job offer to accept.

In addition to requiring decisions, actions also involve risks. Because of their fear of taking risks, some people do not take the action necessary to be successful. If they thought about it, they would realize that they take risks in everything they do, from walking across a street, to applying for a job, to getting married.

One of the reasons that some people avoid taking risks is their fear of failure. Many of the successful students and graduates interviewed for this book said that they did not look at failure as failure, but as a learning opportunity.

We have all engaged in these learning opportunities during our lives. Willie Jolley discussed success and failure in the following excerpt from *A Setback Is a Setup for a Comeback*:

> *You failed many times, although you may not remember. The first time you tried to walk, you fell down. The first time you tried to talk, you hardly made a sound. The first time you dressed yourself, you may have looked like a clown. But you didn't give up! Did you hit the ball the first time you swung a bat? Did you make a cartwheel the first time you tried that? Did you jerk the car the first time you drove a stick? Did you do it perfectly the first time you tried a magic trick? Heavy hitters, the ones who hit the most home runs, also strike out the most, when all is said and done. Babe Ruth struck out 1,330 times, but he also hit 714 home runs. R. H. Macy failed seven times before his store in New York caught on. We all fail sometimes; it is part of success. Just don't stop trying! Don't worry about failure. Worry about the chances you miss when you don't even try.*

To be successful, it is necessary to take risks. According to an old proverb, "Progress always involves risks. You can't steal second while keeping one foot on first." The Olympic gold medalist, Jean Claude Killy, said, "In order to win, you must risk loss."

In setting goals and developing action plans, you can determine the risk involved by determining the following factors:

- The probability of success
- The benefits of success
- The probability of failure
- The consequence of failure

After evaluating each of these factors, you can then determine whether you can decrease the risk and still reach your goal. One of my university professors once stated, "There is risk in crossing the street, but you can lessen it considerably by keeping your eyes open." Reduce the risk, and increase the probability of success.

These "Ten Commandments of Risk Taking," from an unknown source, put it into perspective:

- Thou shalt know that all growth requires risk.
- Thou shalt take into consideration all options.
- Thou shalt be willing to feel uncomfortable and look foolish.
- Thou shalt seek emotional support.
- Thou shalt be willing to pay the price.
- Thou shalt know that it is okay to change your mind.
- Thou shalt know that being rejected is not the worst thing that will happen to you.
- Thou shalt be willing to be without answers.
- Thou shalt know that if you don't try, you will never know.
- Thou shalt know that life is all too short and very precious. Trust your heart.

Sometimes taking action requires problem-solving skills. Some problems are simple and can be solved easily without extensive thought or analysis. Others are more complex and require the use of a process. The following problem-solving process works well for many successful students:

1. Write a synopsis of the current situation, clearly describing the problem. Be as objective as possible.
2. Determine the root cause of the problem. This might start with a list of probable causes. Take into consideration that the problem may be a symptom of another problem and that there can be more than one root cause.
3. Evaluate the root cause to determine what can be changed.
4. Brainstorm alternative solutions for solving the problem.
5. Evaluate each of the alternative solutions.
6. Select and implement the best alternative.

By making decisions, developing action plans, taking risks, and solving problems, successful people have been able to take the action necessary to become even more successful. They know that they need to act in order to accomplish their goals. Taking the first step in an action plan starts the momentum to continued action and to success.

Chapter Six

Stay Focused!

But be flexible

Success requires concentration and focus on our vision, priorities, and goals. However, ours is a time of shrinking concentration spans and less focus. Why are people focusing less now than before? I surveyed a cross-section of students and business people regarding their thoughts on this. Following are some of their opinions of reasons for less concentration and shorter attention spans:

- *We are constantly rushing from one activity to another or from one class to another, without a moment in between. It seems that there is no time to concentrate.*

- *There are so many communication devices that interrupt a person's time. We have cell phones, pagers, call waiting, Internet instant messages, etc.*

- *In our hurry-up world of fragmented communications, we have become accustomed to multi-tasking.*

- *Information is available in so many different sources and in so many different forms today. This includes print (newspapers, magazines, books), broadcast (television and radio), online (Internet and e-mail), and personal interaction.*

- *The television remote control enables us to shorten our attention span. Even the TV news will have three or four things on the screen at the same time.*

- *Television and movies are edited to move quickly. This reflects the faster and faster pace of the world at large.*

- *In my situation, I sometimes have so much on my mind that I have a difficult time clearing it to concentrate on a project. If my mind is cluttered, I become more nervous and frustrated. This then leads to lack of concentration and a shorter attention span. I concentrate better when my mind is relaxed.*

- *Because people are always rushing, they have more difficulty compartmentalizing their lives today. Both my mom and dad bring work home at night and try to do this while spending time with the family, reading the mail, doing the chores around the house, watching TV, and answering phone calls. They are trying to concentrate on several different tasks simultaneously.*

- *People instinctively value and reward instant response today, from fast foods to Web ordering to e-Business. The situation is driven by an information overload world. This sets up a huge pull to be in reactive mode most of the time, making reflection available only to those who can mentally propel themselves out of the fray.*

- *With the use of special effects, today's movies move so quickly, getting adrenaline pumped. With a steady diet of this, we get bored easily with things that might require a longer attention span. Although I have grown up with this and have known it to be a way of life ever since I can remember, I know it hasn't always been this way.*

- *Today, the family system is on the go constantly. This conditions us to move fast and not take time to reflect or to focus.*

Although some of the survey respondents conceded that it is conceivable that shorter attention spans may help people to do several things simultaneously and keep pace with today's rapidly changing world, they all agreed that concentration and focus are ultimately necessary for personal and professional success.

The preceding chapters have highlighted successes of some of the students and graduates interviewed for this book. All of these people have focused on their priorities, goals, and action steps to create success in school and in their lives. When Laurie Windham founded her consulting company, she focused on the niche market that she could best serve. When Kathy White decided to go back to school, she focused on her education and didn't stop until she had her doctorate degree. When Michael Norwood decided to become a full-time author, he focused on writing his first book. In order for Jim Paschal to graduate number one is his class at Arizona State University, he focused on his studies.

Alexander Hamilton once said, "Men give me credit for genius. All the genius I have lies in this: When I have a subject in hand, I study it profoundly. Day and night, it is before me. I explore it in all its bearings. My mind becomes pervaded with it. Then . . . people are pleased to call [the effort that I made] the fruit of genius. It is the fruit of labor and thought." It is the fruit of focus and concentration.

I first met Connie Wolf in Brussels, Belgium, where she was the European vice president of Human Resources and Communications for Dow Corning. She had lived in Europe for almost seven years at that time. In college, she had majored in marketing. During her career, she had been in advertising, communications, consumer marketing, industrial marketing, and human resources. I was just as much impressed with her soft-spoken manner as I was with the breadth of her experience and her business success.

Although Connie's career included many different functions, she always focused on the area in which she was currently assigned. "I liked to be grounded in it," she said. "This helped me to develop the expertise needed to do the job well." Being "grounded" and focusing on your priorities and goals will contribute to your success in college and beyond.

Dr. Jeanne Elnadry is another person who focuses on her priorities and goals and, thus, has achieved success. Her parents encouraged her to be all that she could be. When other girls received nurse's kits for Christmas, Jeanne and her two sisters received doctor's kits. As an adult, Jeanne decided to be a nurse and pursued this career direction. It wasn't until she had been a nurse for several years that she began reminiscing about her childhood doctor's kit and determined that she really wanted to be a doctor.

Once she had made her decision to be a doctor, Jeanne focused on this goal despite the personal hardships she endured along the path. Since she had finished her nursing degree ten years earlier, the other medical school students were younger. Because of this, she thought they were better able to concentrate on their studies. "I had been out of school for quite some time, had not been studying, and wasn't in the mode for that kind of academic work," she said. After having problems with her first exam, she told herself, "I just have to work harder. I can do this." She worked to improve her concentration and never had a problem again. She graduated at the top of her class. She is now a medical doctor specializing in internal medicine. She has a medical clinic in Yuma, Arizona, where her medical practice is so successful that she is not able to accept any new patients.

When asked about the importance of focus and concentration in her life, Jeanne says, "It's very important to me, but it doesn't mean staying focused only on my career. It means staying focused on what is important in my life, which includes career as well as my other priorities."

In today's complicated world, multiple distractions vie for our attention at any given time. The way in which we deal with these distractions determines how well we are able to focus on our goals and priorities. If you will take the time during the next twenty-four hours to observe how you handle distractions, you might have some surprises. During this time period, write each distraction as it occurs. After recording a distraction on paper, write a comment on how you handle this distraction. At the end of the twenty-four hours, review your notes, observe any patterns that may exist, congratulate yourself for the times that you handled the distraction well, and determine where you can make some improvements.

Following are some methods that successful people use to handle distractions:

- Set aside quiet time during the day to focus on your top priorities or action steps. During these quiet times, stay away from the telephone and other sources of interruption, allowing interruptions only for emergencies.

- Decrease the stress in your body and your mind by practicing the relaxation exercise in chapter 2 before you start focusing on a priority or action step.

- Keep a piece of paper and a pen at hand while you are concentrating on a project, such as studying for an exam or writing a paper. When an unrelated thought enters your mind, write it down. These thoughts can be reviewed at a later time.

- Periodically during the next month, repeat the exercise of recording your distractions and the methods that you use to deal with them. Note the progress that you are making in this area.

Bobbie Stevens has accomplished every goal that she has set for herself. She said, "I discovered a process for releasing stress and strengthening the mind/body system. This process has brought me to a totally different level of functioning. It brought me to a higher level of health, energy, and self-confidence." Bobbie's process includes relaxation, visualization, and yoga-type exercises. She stresses that it is important for us to visualize what we want and to keep our attention focused on it, no matter what happens. In her course, Bobbie teaches several methods for improving our ability to focus.

As we can condition, strengthen and tone our bodies, we can also condition and strengthen our minds to improve our concentration and focus. The keys to increasing our ability to focus are practice and repetition. The following exercises will help to improve your ability to concentrate and to focus on your priorities and goals:

1. Focus on an object.

Select an object in the room that is pleasing to you. This could be a painting, a sculpture, a piece of furniture, etc. Move your chair so that you can see the object clearly without any physical strain. Sit comfortably with your back straight. Now fix your eyes on the object, and leave them there. Focus your full attention on the object for three minutes. Do not let other thoughts distract you during the three minutes. If your mind starts to wander, bring it back to focus on the object.

Keep a piece of paper and a pencil on hand during this exercise. Each time your mind wanders from the object, you can then make a tick mark on the paper. If you are like most of us, there will be lots of tick marks on your paper after you complete the exercise for the first time. However, the number of tick marks should decrease as you strengthen your ability to focus by repeating this exercise during the next several days.

2. Candle concentration.

Bobbie Stevens teaches the candle concentration exercise in her course. In order to do this one, you will need a lighted candle. Start by sitting comfortably, as described previously, and place the lighted candle on a table about three feet in front of you. Gaze directly into the flame of the candle (blinking as necessary) for two minutes. Then close your eyes, and press the palms of your hands lightly against your eyelids. When you close your eyes, you will retain the image of the flame. Concentrate on that image, and do not let the flame wander or disappear. If it should disappear, bring it back simply by looking for it (keeping your eyes closed). Keep your palms pressed against your closed eyes for an additional two minutes.

This exercise not only helps to improve focus and concentration, but it also brings restfulness and relaxation. This, in turn, helps to relieve stress. By decreasing stress, a person is better able to focus.

3. Physical exercise.

Another way to clear the mind and increase the ability to concentrate is through physical exercise. In the past, I had days that it seemed like it would be a major effort to walk to my car and drive home after work. I would feel so tired that I thought I needed a nap. The fact was that I really needed some physical exercise. After sitting in an office all day, making decisions, and handling major problems, I felt tired. My ability to focus seemed to be gone for the day. At first, it surprised me how a twenty-minute walk could make such a big difference and eliminate these symptoms.

Physical exercise allows the mind to relax. It releases stress, which is a major barrier to concentration. In addition, it helps to strengthen the body.

* * * * *

In *Brain Building*, Marilyn vos Savant says, "When there is a severe decline in memory and mental function, it is usually caused by such diseases as Alzheimer's which affects only 20 percent of the very old. Most of the other decline, the kind that people tend to fret about as they age, is now believed to be caused by the lack of mental exercise."

My ability to focus has definitely helped me to accomplish my goals and to enjoy success in all areas of my life. My European position was a developmental assignment, which allowed me to learn as well as to accomplish objectives which I was given the liberty to recommend to the company. During the two years I spent in Europe, it would have been very easy to get a flavor of European cultures and business life and still not show concrete results for my efforts in my job there. When I first knew that I would have the assignment, I decided that I was going to focus on four areas and to make major contributions in these areas. I selected the following four areas:

- Sales and marketing productivity, which involved restructuring internal job descriptions to best meet customer requirements. This would be demonstrated by conducting a pilot in one business unit in one country.

- Sales support systems, which included introducing computers to sales personnel to assist them in becoming more effective and more efficient in their jobs.

- Customer satisfaction measurement, which also involved the implementation of improvements, based on customer requirements.

- Balanced scorecard development, which included various measures that would be used to determine the progress of all business units in Europe.

For each of these areas of concentration, I established teams, conducted research, developed plans, and started implementation. Of course, there were other projects that came up while I was in Europe that threatened my ability to focus on my selected priorities. Some of them were quite attractive, and I found myself wishing that I was two people and could do more; however, I was able to analyze the priority in each case and to concentrate on the established priorities. At the end of the two years, I had accomplished my objectives and was promoted to a new position in the company.

Along with increasing your ability to focus comes a paradox. Even though it is extremely important to focus on your goals and action steps, it is also important to be flexible. In some cases, we may have conflicting priorities. In others, several of our priorities might need our attention simultaneously. During these times, an analysis will help to determine the most important thing to be doing right now.

Jill Lublin strongly believes in the power of focus. She says that one of the things that has significantly contributed to her success is that she has mastered an ongoing focus. She says, "I am very much focused on what I need to do to create more of who I truly am, to express myself more fully, and to give the gift of who I am to this world." In her work, she currently has three major priorities—speaking internationally, serving her clients as a consultant, and developing and keeping *GoodNews Media* (her television show) strong. She focuses on each of these individually, as well as collectively.

Keeping in mind the importance of flexibility, I recommend that you work on focusing on your visions, priorities, goals, and action steps. In addition to increasing your concentration, this will feed your subconscious mind the information it needs to help you to be successful.

Before the 1993 Superbowl, Dallas Cowboys coach Jimmy Johnson gave his team a pep talk. He told them that, if he laid a two-by-four plank on the floor, each of them would walk across it and not fall. The reason for this would be that their focus would be on walking the plank. "But if I put the same two-by-four ten stories high between two buildings," said Johnson, "only a few would make it." This would be because the focus would be on falling. He told his team not to focus on the crowd, the media, or the possibility of losing. Instead, they were to focus on each play of the game, just as if it were a good practice session. The Dallas Cowboys won the game 52 to 17.

Stephanie Kane says, "It's easy to let your goals fall to the wayside or say you'll do it when the 'time is right' or when you have the money. Do it. Do it right now. Take baby steps or integrate daily actions into your routine to execute your master plan or remind you of what you want."

If you focus on winning, you will win. If you focus on accomplishing your goals, you will accomplish your goals. If you focus on success, you will be successful. The key is to focus and to continue to improve your ability to focus through the exercises in this chapter.

Chapter Seven

Remain Positive, No Matter What!

A winning attitude can open doors

Thoughts direct energy. Positive thoughts create positive energy and results, and negative thoughts create negative energy and results. If you expect the best, you are more likely to achieve it.

In order to see this for yourself, look around you at the positive, optimistic people that you know. Are they successful? Chances are they are enjoying life and creating what they want in their lives.

Now look at the negative, pessimistic people that you know. How successful are they? My guess is that they are not happy with their lives.

How happy are you with your life? Are you as successful in school and in life as you would like to be? How positive are you? Do you look at problems as problems, or do you look at them as opportunities? Oil magnate and philanthropist John D. Rockefeller maintained that he tried to turn every disaster into an opportunity, and it certainly paid off for him!

We all have problems and challenges in life, and many people feel defeated by these. Our attitude and the way that we handle our problems and challenges will contribute to our success or lack thereof. Dr. Norman Vincent Peale addresses this in the following excerpt from *The Power of Positive Thinking:*

> *Altogether too many people are defeated by the everyday problems of life. They go struggling, perhaps even whining, through their days with a sense of dull resentment at what they consider the "bad breaks" life has given them. In a sense, there may be such a thing as "the breaks" in this life, but there is also a spirit and method by which we can control and even determine those breaks. It is a pity that people should let themselves be defeated by the problems, cares, and difficulties of human existence, and it is also quite unnecessary.*
>
> *In saying this, I certainly do not ignore or minimize the hardships and tragedies of the world, but neither do I allow them to dominate. You can permit obstacles to control your mind to the point where they are uppermost and thus become the dominating factors in your thought pattern. By learning how to cast them from the mind, by refusing to become mentally subservient to them, and by channeling spiritual power through your thoughts, you can rise above obstacles which ordinarily might defeat you. You need be defeated only if you are willing to be.*

As I interviewed successful students and graduates for this book, I asked them about their experiences with failure in their lives. Some would say that they had never failed. Others would hesitate before answering, as if they were trying of think of an example. Finally they would mention something that had happened—losing a spelling bee in elementary school, failing a test, scoring a goal for the opponent, etc. They all maintained that they perceived these occurrences as learning opportunities rather than failures. Many of them talked about the lessons they had learned that enabled them to accomplish greater goals. Some said that it was because of their failures that they were able to become successful.

William James said, "The greatest discovery of my generation is that human beings can alter their lives by altering their attitudes of mind."

My personal experience validates this philosophy. Before I decided to alter my attitude, I spent much time in hospitals. Early in my career, I was diagnosed with a serious heart condition. My doctor ordered me to quit work, as he said that my heart condition was too serious for me to contend with the stress of a job. At the time, I was twenty-nine years old and was concerned about the possibility of not living to see my thirtieth birthday. I was even more concerned about the possibility of not having the opportunity to raise my children, who were then eight and two. Even though I enjoyed my work, I chose to follow the doctor's orders.

During the next several months, more was discovered about my particular heart condition. With the use of a combination of four different medications, the condition was under control. I was gradually able to return to work, first part time and then full time. However, worry and concern about the heart condition still permeated my existence.

Less than two weeks after returning to work full time, I had an experience that helped me to realize the power of thought. While sitting at my desk, I started hearing a constant ringing sound and was not able to determine the source of this sound. As the ringing started to get louder, I decided to discuss it with a colleague. When I arrived at my colleague's desk, he was not there. His phone was ringing, so I answered it with the intent of taking a message for him. To my alarm, the voice at the other end of the line was garbled. This was a sign to me that the ringing I had been hearing was coming from inside my head, and something was terribly wrong. I politely told the person on the phone that we had a bad connection and suggested that she call back in a few minutes when my colleague was due to return. To verify that I was correct in the diagnosis of the problem, I dialed the phone number of the recorded time and temperature message. The sound from the message was also garbled.

My next sensation was a light-headed feeling. I called my doctor, who suggested that I have someone drive me home, that I go directly to bed, and that I call him the next morning if I had not improved. By the time I got home, I was completely deaf in my right ear. Thinking that this would pass, I waited until morning to call the doctor. At that point, I was so dizzy that I could not lift my head off my pillow without being sick to my stomach. I remember being barely conscious as someone wheeled a gurney from the hospital emergency room to the back of the station wagon where I was lying. I heard a voice saying, "Be careful with her. She is very, very sick."

I lay in a hospital bed for almost three weeks, not able to move because of the extreme dizziness. Once I could get up, it took months to learn to walk a straight line again. I never regained my hearing. The doctors explained that a blood vessel in my inner ear had "shorted out," causing the inner ear to die and destroying the balance mechanism. They attributed this to stress. In looking back, I know now that the stress was self-inflicted by my worries about my health.

After a while, I was again able to return to work but was in and out of hospitals for several years for various health problems, including asthma, pneumonia, heart irregularities, and abdominal surgeries. When I finally started to think positively about my health and my life, I became healthy. I am still deaf in the right ear but have learned to compensate for this. My asthma is under control, and I no longer need to take medication for my heart. There definitely is power in positive thinking! I had altered my health, and my life, by altering my "attitude of mind."

Following are nine methods for improving one's attitude and outlook. They have contributed to my success and to the success of those I have coached and mentored, as well as the people I interviewed for this book.

I. Refrain from the three C's.

During the course that Bobbie Stevens developed, she and her husband, Dean, teach the "square tongue rule." Dean states this rule quite simply when he advises course participants to refrain from the three C's, described long ago by Dale Carnegie, which are complaining, criticizing, and condemning. He recommends that participants become aware of each time they complain, criticize, or condemn. He then suggests that, while taking the course, they gently bite the end of their tongue as a reminder each time they engage in one of the three C's. He jokingly adds that, if the tip of the tongue is bitten too many times, it might be bitten off; hence the square tongue rule!

When I first heard about the square tongue rule, I almost dismissed it. My initial thought was that I don't complain, criticize, or condemn. However, since I was committed to getting as much out of this course as possible, I decided to follow Dean's instructions for the next week. As I became more aware of my words and thoughts, I learned that I wasted a great deal of time making critical remarks. At first I would justify my remarks to myself by thinking, "I'm not criticizing, but just stating a fact." I discovered how easy it is to justify our thoughts, words, and actions. It became apparent that I needed to make some adjustments in my thinking.

After some analysis, I realized that not only do the three C's rob our time, but they also drag us down into a spiral of negativity. The messages, which they send to the subconscious mind, inhibit our success. Although it took some time for me to progress in eliminating the three C's from my life, I discovered that it was well worth the effort.

During the next week, I suggest that you become aware of each time that you complain, criticize, or condemn. When you catch yourself engaging in any of these C's, ask yourself what you would need to do in order to restate or eliminate your current thought or words. If you are like I was, you might discover that you are complaining, criticizing, or condemning more than you would have thought you were. However, as you observe this and restate your thoughts, you'll soon find that you are engaging in the three C's less often. By doing this, you will be eliminating the negative energy that is generated by complaining, criticizing, and condemning.

By eliminating complaining, criticizing, and condemning, we become more positive. On the mental level, positive attracts positive, and negative attracts negative. Positive thoughts help to attract more positive experiences into our lives. This begins an upward spiral. As we begin to see things in a more positive way, we become more positive. As we become more positive, we increase our potential for success.

2. Eliminate worry from your life.

Just as most successful people do not waste time complaining, criticizing, and condemning, they also do not waste time worrying. They realize that worry generates negative energy, and it does not make the source of the worry any better.

There are so many things that can be sources of worry in our lives. You might worry about whether you will pass a test, get a paper finished on time, or if you will have a date for a special occasion. Many of us were conditioned to worry, and we just kept worrying our way into college and beyond. After college graduation, the worries might be about getting a job in your field, whether your boss will be happy with your work, or having enough money to pay your bills. Your worries might be about things as simple as whether you will be on time for an appointment or have enough gas in the car to get to the nearest station.

Before my husband, Cliff, and I were engaged, I was worried that he may have another heart attack. When I didn't hear from him at the beginning of a day, it would affect my thoughts on other things. Of course, Cliff sensed my anxiety, and this did not enhance our relationship. When I finally decided to stop worrying, our relationship blossomed, my mind became more clear for positive thoughts, I became more productive, people noticed my more positive attitude, and I was promoted at work. I learned that I could care, but that did not mean that I needed to worry.

Many of us have serious concerns, such as life-threatening illnesses in our families. Worrying does not cure an illness, and we ourselves can become sick from the worry. Once we decide to stop worrying, we are better able to handle a situation that might have been the object of our worry. During the next week, you might want to observe whether you are spending time worrying. If you discover that you are worrying, you can then give some thought to the things you can do to continue caring and stop worrying.

3. Put on a happy face.

Have you ever noticed how people seem to want to please you more when you smile at them? To me, they appear to be more friendly and outgoing. When I realized this, I started to consciously observe people's reactions as I smiled at them while walking through the long corridors of 3M's office complex. I discovered that, whenever I smiled, the recipient of the smile would return the smile. This, in turn, lifted my spirits. As a result, my smile became more genuine as I met the next person.

In her course, Bobbie Stevens teaches the power of positive thinking. After my management group decided to participate in the course, a colleague told me of a conversation she had with the manager of another department. The colleague had mentioned to the manager that my group would be attending this course. She was amused by the reaction when the manager said, "Oh no! This means that we will have ten more 'Joans' running around, smiling at people, looking through their rose-colored glasses, and getting all of the promotions! I wish I could be like that."

The truth is that she could be like that. The formula is simple. As one of my philosopher friends said, "We don't see things as they are; we see them as we are." If we convey an attitude of happiness and show this through our smiles, we will see the same thing in other people. This is illustrated by the story of a man who traveled from town to town looking for a place to start his business. As he went into one town, he asked a resident about the type of people who lived there. The wise resident asked him what type of people lived in the town that he was leaving. The man replied that the people were unfriendly, argumentative, and uncooperative. The resident replied that the man would find the people in this town the same as the ones in the town the man had left. The next day, another man arrived in the same town and asked the same resident about the type of people who lived in the town. The resident asked this man the same question about the type of people in the town he was leaving. This man replied that the people were friendly, cooperative, and always willing to help. The resident answered his question by saying that he would find that the people in this town were the same as the ones in the town that he had left. Both men had visited the same town, had talked with the same resident, and had asked the same question; however they had received different answers, depending on how each of them saw things.

What type of people have you met at your college or university? Are they friendly and outgoing, or are they unfriendly and uncooperative? If they are the former, that's great. However, if they are the latter, I encourage you to try my experiment and put on a happy face.

4. Look for the good in everything.

At a 3M meeting several years ago, I met a woman named Mary, who was the ultimate for making lemonade when life dealt her lemons. I had never before known anyone with an attitude as positive as hers. At the beginning of the meeting, each of us introduced ourselves and gave a synopsis of the reasons for our participation in this series of meetings. Mary had recently moved to St. Paul, Minnesota, from Washington, D.C. Her position in Washington had been eliminated. She told us that, even though she had enjoyed her job there, losing it was a wonderful opportunity to look at other positions and to determine what she would like to do next. She found a position in Minnesota and rented an apartment about twenty-five miles from the office where she worked. She even talked about how fantastic it was to have an hour-long commute to and from her new job, as she was able to see much of the city and to listen to motivating tapes while she was driving.

Others who heard her told me later that they didn't think Mary was "for real." As I got to know her, though, I realized that she was truly genuine. As others in the group began to know her, they also realized it and strived to be more like her. They recognized that she was attracting positive into her life through her attitude. When I was hiring people for my next new department, Mary was one of the first people I hired. Her attitude and enthusiasm were contagious, and she contributed significantly to the success of this department.

In *Golden Nuggets*, Sir John Templeton says, "By choosing to look for the good in all situations, we can place our attention on workable solutions to problems, rather than focusing on what we perceive as wrong."

I once attended a class given by a chiropractor who had developed an excellent chiropractic procedure, which not only included adjustments, but also nutrition and "forgiveness." During the class sessions, he discussed the subconscious mind and the fact that thought precedes action, even physical action/reaction within our bodies.

This wise doctor of chiropractic explained that the secret to recovery in many of these cases was forgiveness. Sometimes unknowingly, we carry grudges for something that happened to us at sometime during our lives. If we do some serious soul-searching, we can determine if there might be someone that we have not forgiven. In class, we learned the three steps of forgiveness:

1. Forgive the person who may have wronged us.
2. Forgive ourselves for carrying the grudge, whether it was intentional or unintentional.
3. Look for the good in whatever it was that happened to us. This is the most difficult step, but it is necessary for the process to work.

There were some people in the class who were very ill and had traveled to doctors throughout the country in search of cures for their illnesses. It seemed to me that I saw miracles occurring that week when many of these ill people were relieved of their symptoms. In following up after the class, I learned that, for most of these people, the symptoms never returned.

During the class, I determined that part of the reason I have had abdominal cramps most of my life went back to a violent situation that I had witnessed when I was twelve years old. I had not realized that I had carried a grudge against someone for causing this situation. Even though the perpetrator was no longer living, I was still carrying this grudge, and the violent act was still living in my subconscious mind. After engaging in the three steps of forgiveness for twenty-four hours, I still had abdominal cramps. It was then that I realized that I was merely going through the motions. I had to do some real work to genuinely forgive and to look for some good in the violent situation that had occurred. This gave me an opportunity to not only forgive, but also to grow. Since that time, I have rarely experienced abdominal cramps.

Looking for the good in all experiences contributes to building a more positive attitude. The following excerpt from Dr. Dean Portinga's paper, "Pronounce All Things Good," helps to explain this.

> *The act of affirming the good is a very powerful factor, reflecting itself in all areas of our lives. . . . The thought of good dissolves all kinds of beliefs in burdens. This thought of good dissolves suspicion, doubt, fear, ingratitude, self-pity, grudges, sadness, hurt feelings, impatience, hatred, condemnation, revenge, and bitterness. All kinds of negative thoughts that cause burdens in thought, body, and experience can be cleared up with such a simple statement as, "Only good is going on."*

> *When you speak the word "good," you are*
> *releasing power. The word "good" is creative.*
> *Good is created as fast as good thoughts and*
> *words are spoken. When you speak forth the word*
> *"good," you evolve, stir up, and release good to*
> *manifest.*
>
> *The word "good" is also self-increasing.*
> *When you speak forth words of good, you not only*
> *create good, but that good continues to create*
> *more good. It is self-multiplying. Thus, by*
> *speaking words of good, you first create and then*
> *increase all things good in your experience. This*
> *includes the physical well-being, financial well-*
> *being, and the well-being of human relationships.*
> *Good is another name for strength and*
> *power. . . . You can confidently expect good*
> *things to happen when you take your stand and*
> *pronounce everything good!*

5. Know that you can do it.

A positive attitude, combined with self-affirmation, contributes to success. If you continually tell yourself that you can accomplish your objectives, you significantly increase the likelihood of doing just that. Although teachers told Michael Norwood his grammar was poor, he knew he was a good writer. He pursued his passion and has since written and published three books that have enhanced thousands of people's lives.

Annie O'Connor, who graduated from St. Louis University and Northwestern University, is the corporate director, Musculoskeletal Practice at Rehabilitation Institute of Chicago. While a full-time physical therapy student in college, she played three sports and enjoyed socializing both on and off campus. She knew that she would be able to handle all of her priorities and accomplish her objectives. Some of the things that have helped her to become most successful are following her passion for life, helping others, and maintaining a positive attitude. She said, "Our bodies are chemically reactive and respond to positive reinforcement. Positive attitudes produce positive chemical reactions, and negative attitudes produce negative chemical reactions."

As an artillery battery executive officer and safety office for the 1st U.S. Army Space Battalion, Nicholas Kahler was deployed to Iraq, knowing that many American soldiers who went there would never return. Although it was difficult to leave his wife and two-year-old daughter, he maintained a positive attitude and knew he could survive. He said, "A positive attitude allows you to make the best of terrible situations, encourages others in the face of danger, and changes cynicism into a better way of doing things. Having a positive attitude helped me get through things like Thanksgiving in Iraq, family tragedy, and financial stress."

Dr. Jeanne Elnadry was painfully shy as a child. "I did something about it when I was in junior high school," she said. "I remember walking down a hallway one day and feeling so out of place, as teenagers often do. It was like a light went on in my head. I realized that if I wanted to change the situation, I was the one who had to do it. It would not happen by itself. So, during the course of those years, I ran the school newspaper. I started out as a reporter and learned how to talk with people. I joined the drill team and eventually became its captain. These were structured activities that helped me to deal with the shyness and get beyond it. I think that the attitude of trying to get beyond a difficulty is what kept me going."

Once she realized why she felt out of place, Jeanne knew that she could do what was necessary to overcome her shyness. She is now a successful physician.

Know that you can accomplish your objectives. If you're shy like Jeanne was, it might mean that you need to stretch yourself outside of your comfort zone. If your objective is better grades, it might mean changing your study habits. If you want to be a starter on the varsity team, it might mean more training and more practice.

If you know that you can accomplish your objectives and you commit yourself to take the necessary steps, you will be successful.

6. Laugh.

A growing number of doctors and nurses are studying the healing power of laughter. Various studies have indicated that laughter can stimulate a hormone that increases immune response. I read about this shortly before I injured my back on a business trip. Since the back injury was so painful, I went to see a doctor after I arrived at my destination. He prescribed medication for pain and to relax my muscles. He also suggested that I stay in bed for the next two days. I took the medication immediately and returned to my hotel. The back pain was worse the next day, so much so that it prevented me from attending my meetings. I was in bed feeling sorry for myself when I remembered the passage I had read about laughter. I began to laugh. I flipped through the TV channels looking for a situation comedy. I thought of funny stories, and I laughed more. The more I laughed, the better I felt. I could still feel the pain, but it was no longer dominating my thoughts. By the next day, I was able to attend meetings. The pain was almost gone, even though I had stopped taking the pain medication.

There is healing power in laughter, and this power can heal us mentally and emotionally, as well as physically. Laughter helps to release stress. After an intense study session, a good laugh can revitalize you. It brings with it a good feeling, a feeling of lightness, a feeling of joy. It can also be invigorating to spend time with people who have a sense of humor, as it is difficult to have a good sense of humor and a bad attitude.

We once had a speaker come to our office and talk to the employees about stress management. He was a medical doctor but was dressed as a clown. As he walked to the front of the room, some of the employees were wondering how this silly person was able to come to our conservative company to speak to us. By the middle of his talk, everyone in the audience was laughing so hard that several of them had tears running down their faces. At the end of his speech, the doctor/clown received a standing ovation. Our departmental productivity increased significantly over the next several days because of his impact.

There is power in laughter. The great entertainer, Bob Hope, said, "I have seen what a good laugh can do. It can transform tears into hope."

7. Value other people.

Each individual on this earth is a miracle. Each of us has unique skills, talents, and aptitudes. We all live in a connected universe and contribute to the growth of one another. We are partners in the creation of good for all of us. As we show respect for others as individuals, we, in turn, gain respect.

William Penn wrote, "I expect to pass through life but once. If therefore, there be any kindness I can show, or any good thing that I can to do to any fellow being, let me do it now, and not defer or neglect it, as I shall not pass this way again." Although this was written a long time ago, it helps me to get my life back in perspective each time I read it.

People are precious, even those who seem to be cross and ornery and those who seem to stand in the way of our achieving our objectives. If we value them and show that we care about them as people, we might be surprised at the difference we will see in them. By adjusting our attitude toward them, we might just see a change in their attitude toward us.

Popular motivational speaker Zig Ziglar says, "You can have everything in life you want, if you will just help enough other people get what they want." Many people just want to know that they are valued and that you respect and care about them.

Connie Wolf, former European vice president of Human Resources and Communications for Dow Corning, advises people who want to create success in their lives to "be kind." She adheres to the premise that relationships come before outcomes, materialism, and "being right." She stresses that it helps maintain our relationships if we ask ourselves if the current situation will matter tomorrow, next week, or next year.

Another tip from Connie is to make a difference in others' lives. She says that if you believe that you can make a difference for just one person each day through a smile, a kind word, or a helping hand, you yourself will benefit.

Jeff Notto says, "Positive attitude means having a good outlook, which can also be viewed as a good sense of self-worth and security. When you have a positive attitude, people will recognize this and want to be around you. Good relationships are essential in a business career, and a positive attitude is important in developing and maintaining these relationships."

It takes very little to touch another person's life, to let people know that you value them. A word of encouragement might make a difference to someone who thinks that it is a lonely and uncaring world. By valuing other people and showing that we care, we are developing a more positive attitude in ourselves.

8. Set an example.

All of us are seen and observed by other people on a daily basis. As we become more successful, it seems that we are "on stage" even more often. You have probably noticed this as you have observed the starters on your college teams or those who play the lead in the school musicals. Because of my position at 3M, I felt that I was representing the company whenever I was out in public. I would not always know if someone around me would recognize me. Nevertheless, I felt it was important to live my personal standards, regardless of where I might be. People know that I am a positive, optimistic woman. By maintaining this positive attitude, I know I have influenced many others through my example.

Business and management guru Peter Drucker, said, "Your first and foremost job as a leader is to raise your own energy level and then to help orchestrate the energies of those around you." This energy includes attitude. It also applies outside of business, as all of you have the opportunity to set an example in your school and in your family.

9. Give back to society.

Most of the successful people, who participated in my interviews, talked about the importance of "giving back." Gayle Crowell gives back when she donates her speaker fees to charity. Jeff Notto, and his wife, Carol, give back when they lead marriage ministry programs.

William H. Danforth, founder of Ralston Purina and author of *I Dare You!*, said, "Catch a passion for helping others, and a richer life will come back to you!"

Giving to others reaps rewards for the giver, even though the giver is not giving for the sake of personal reward. Ralph Waldo Emerson said, "It is one of the most beautiful compensations of this life that no man can sincerely try to help another without helping himself."

* * * * *

When we are in the midst of challenges and crises, it is sometimes difficult to be optimistic and positive. However, it helps to remember that positive attitudes can open the door to opportunities.

Throughout my career, I have interviewed nearly one thousand individuals for jobs within the various organizations that I have managed. Before I interview potential employees for a position, I develop a list of criteria and standard questions to ask each interviewee. Regardless of the position, the number one criterion for the position is "attitude," which is even more important to me than whether the person has the exact technical skills needed for the position. If the interviewee has a positive attitude, I know that he or she can be trained, if need be, on most of the other skills needed for the position. By looking at attitude as the top criterion, I have been able to develop departments that have achieved the following:

- High level of productivity and creativity
- Consistent exceeding of objectives
- High level of morale
- Effective team-building

- High level of respect from others in the company
- Low absenteeism
- Low turnover

The people in these departments have worked hard, and they have worked smart. They have also had fun in doing this. As a result, others in the company have often asked for transfers into these departments. This is due largely to the attitude of the employees.

A positive attitude definitely opens doors. It has for me and for each of the successful people that I have met in my life. It will for you, too.

Chapter Eight

Live Your Life with Integrity!

Without this, other efforts lack importance

When I lived and worked in Europe, I had two bosses, one in France where I lived and the other in Belgium, the location of our European headquarters. Both bosses were women, two of the three highest-ranking women at 3M at that time. I felt fortunate to have the opportunity to learn from these two business giants and was enormously flattered at one point when one of them complimented me by saying that she could always count on my dedication and integrity. She added that, no matter what I say I am going to do, she knows that I will do it. I felt that was the best compliment that anyone could have paid me. From that day forward, I wanted to make sure that I would always live up to it.

Maintaining integrity is not easy for many of us. During part of my life, everyday temptations to alter the truth were difficult for me to overcome. When I was in my early thirties, I decided to take up the game of golf. During my first year on the golf course, my scores were sometimes almost twice as high as those of some of my playing partners. Since I was the ultimate perfectionist, this was extremely embarrassing to me. After each hole as we called out our scores, I would be tempted to lower my score by one or two strokes so that it would not sound quite as bad as it was. A tempting voice inside of me would say, "Make up a number. They probably can't count that high anyway." I would think about it and finally answer the voice, saying, "But I would know it, and I am the one who has to live with myself." The everyday temptations for us to be out of integrity are probably stronger than any other temptations we receive.

Dan Love, a graduate of Stanford University, says that he was not a successful student. "My academic achievements were capped by graduating after four years but with no zeal for what I had learned," he said. "I embarked on a major, encouraged by prep school faculty, for which I had only partial aptitude. My second major was a default. I was lost and unprepared to ask directions. Personally, I was marking time and took few, if any, of the opportunities Stanford and its locale offered."

Dan is now retired after a career focusing on business strategy and marketing, which he applied to aviation, travel, and tourism. He worked for aviation consultants, airlines, two start-up airlines (which he founded), a major mountain resort, and the state of Colorado as its tourism director.

An open and honest person, Dan says that personal integrity was a strong contributor to success in his career. He says that the most important steps he took in his aviation career were a combination of luck and self-direction. "My choice of aviation was based on my search for a start-up industry in which I could make a difference and be a part of its evolution," he said. "In 1960, when I graduated, only 10 percent of U.S. commercial passenger traffic was carried by all airlines combined. Airline travel was an adventure spawned by the availability of World War II technology and pilots. Is it any wonder it was attractive to a person with a strategic mind and attracted to technology? Travel and tourism was a natural outgrowth of my aviation experience, coupled with a passion for the natural and historic attractions of Colorado. Starting two airlines was an extension of my understanding of the competitive structure of the industry."

Dan also demonstrates integrity in his priorities in life, which are to derive satisfaction from whatever he does, to be considerate of others and the world in which we live, and to be thoughtful about the choices he makes.

All of the interviewees for this book agree that integrity is of utmost importance to their success. In a survey of additional successful people, I asked them to rate the importance of personal integrity on a scale of one to five, with "five" meaning most important. They all rated it a "five." One said, "Six!" Another said, "Five-five-five!" Following are some of the comments from my interviewees. I hope they will serve to inspire you as you give some consideration to where you see yourself on the personal integrity scale.

- "My sense of personal integrity has kept me honest, hard-working, and loyal to my commitments. If I can't feel good about what I'm doing, I don't do it. I try to put the common good ahead of my own personal interests, although I have learned that I have to look out for myself sometimes. I try to measure my decisions by what I would be willing to have brought to public scrutiny. If all my friends and family were to know what I am thinking, what I am doing, what I am hoping for at any given time, would I be comfortable or feel ashamed? I believe we will all someday answer for the way we lived our lives. That belief has a great impact on my attitude and my actions and has forged a strong commitment to personal integrity. I believe I have been rewarded for that integrity by having been given opportunities for leadership and positions of trust." (K. D. Taylor, associate dean, Utah Valley State College)

- "Personal integrity has been the standard to which I have compared the actions that have been requested of me. If they did not fit, other arrangements had to be made, or I left the company. I feel that personal integrity has been my guide and safety but more than that, it has given me the courage to move into other areas of endeavor which have proven to be satisfying and have resulted in continued personal growth. Personal integrity is the governing principle of my life." (Keith Geilman, sales manager)

- "Personal integrity is being true to myself and to others. The right thought, the right action, and the right motivation drive my ability to perform well in my job and allow balance in my life. (I certainly sleep well at night!)" (Rebecca O'Neill, attorney)

- "Personal integrity is vital to my success. I need to be known as someone who moves in an ethical and professional way. My industry is cluttered with unethical people, and for me to rise to the top, integrity is essential. (Becky Creighton, self-employed real estate investor)

- "You need to be who you are, to be honest, to feel good about yourself, and to be true to yourself. At the end of the day, personal integrity will carry you the whole way." (Gayle Crowell, former president, publicly-traded company)

- "Part of personal integrity is doing your best. Part of it is being honest. Part of it is being true to your values. People will not remember what you did or what you said, but they will always remember how they felt when they were with you. The way we treat other people is part of our integrity. To succeed, you need to be trustworthy. If we are not honest and we don't keep our integrity, we can't be trustworthy. Another part of it is that sometimes we might be criticized. If we take responsibility for a mistake, a lot of criticism melts away. Part of integrity is taking responsibility for what we have done and acknowledging it." (Dr. Jeanne Elnadry, physician)

- "Nothing is worth sacrificing your integrity. It is extremely important to be true to yourself. You need to know what is right for you and to stay on that track." (Dr. Bobbie Stevens, author, speaker, personal development specialist)

> - "Integrity is doing what I say I will do and trying to make that almost my whole being. It is about the calls, the follow-up, the calling back if someone is not there, and the follow-through to completion of a task or project. It launched my success the first ten years when I was more of an individual contributor. After that, personal integrity also became very important in order for people to want to follow me and to do big things." (Dr. Kathy Brittain White, executive vice president and chief information officer, major health care company)

One of the interviewees talked about how she had learned the importance of integrity from some traumatic childhood experiences. As a child, she was sexually abused by a relative, and she learned later that he had also abused all of her female cousins. From this horrible experience, she learned that it is very important to be believed and trusted. She said, "Probably the worse thing that can happen now is for someone not to believe me. I have high personal integrity. Even though I will position things to get the best play and achieve the best results, I tell the truth. The reality of how I was treated as a child is so bizarre. Those things are just not normal, and they should not happen. When I look at how everything else was so phenomenal in my life, I wasn't going to let this get to me. On the other hand, it has an impact on how I live my life. Honesty and integrity are so very, very important to me."

What does integrity mean to you? In the case of my golf score, I considered integrity to be an honesty issue. Although honesty contributes to integrity, there are more aspects to integrity than just telling the truth. Integrity is unique for each of us, and most integrity challenges start with details. We might receive early warning signals that we just ignore until they have become a problem.

As you are thinking about your level of integrity, ask yourself the following questions:

- Do I tell the truth?
- Is my word my bond?

- Do my promises have value?
- Do I do what I say I am going to do?
- Am I committed to commitment?

In *The Portable Coach*, Coach University founder Thomas J. Leonard makes the following statement about integrity:

> *Everyone, myself included, should be open to micro or macro improvements in how "together" they are. It could be as simple as installing a system that keeps you as up to date as possible in paperwork and organization, so the right responses are always generated quickly.*
>
> *The same applies to being on the curve, instead of behind it, when it comes to handling taxes, having adequate insurance, being current on registrations and debt repayment, being available in the present moment for key relationships and agreements, and staying rooted in truthfulness and forthrightness.*
>
> *Integrity is more than just honesty. It's about being integrated, so that all the parts of your life and yourself are cooperating smoothly to honor your best interests. Since we ultimately can't possess anything more important than our good name, any upgrade to your integrity will eventually be an addition to your well-being.*

Integrity is the result of having the following three conditions in one's life:

- **Resolution of all important matters**
  This includes the correction of any wrongs, making any personal changes necessary to ensure one's life works well, and fully handling every task and job that one decides to do.
- **Alignment and balance in life**
  Alignment, in this case, means that a person's goals are aligned with their values and priorities, their actions are based on what

is true for them, and their commitments are aligned with their vision or purpose in life.

- **Responsibility**

  In speaking about integrity, the word "responsibility" means being responsible for that which occurs in one's life. This includes handling whatever happens and making necessary adjustments to prevent this type of problem in the future. A responsible person does not blame, complain, or point fingers at other people, but just handles the situation.

* * * * *

By the results you are seeing in your life, it is usually fairly easy to determine whether you are "in integrity" or "out of integrity." When you are "in integrity," you experience fewer problems, have consistent feelings of peace and well-being, and react to situations and other people very little. When you are "out of integrity," you are more likely to become distressed and irritable and to blame and criticize others. The more we live our lives with integrity, the more harmony and beauty we will encounter.

In *The Six Pillars of Self Esteem*, Nathaniel Branden says, "One of the greatest deceptions is to tell oneself, 'Only I will know.' Only I will know that I am a liar; only I will know that I deal unethically with people who trust me; only I will know that I have no intention of honoring my promise. The implication is that my judgment is unimportant and that only the judgment of others counts."

In *100 Ways to Motivate Yourself*, Steve Chandler comments on Nathaniel Branden's quote:

> *Branden's writing on personal integrity is*
> *inspiring because it's directed at creating a*
> *happier and stronger self, not at a universal*
> *appeal for morality.*
>
> *One of the ways we describe a work of art that*
> *is sloppy or unfinished is as "a mess." The*
> *problem with lying, or lying by omission, is that it*

> *leaves everything incomplete—in a mess. Truth*
> *always completes the picture—any picture. And*
> *when a picture is complete, whole and integrated,*
> *we see it as 'beautiful'. . . . Truth and beauty*
> *become impossible to separate.*
>
> *Truth leads you to a more confident level in*
> *your relationships with others and yourself. It*
> *diminishes fear and increases your sense of*
> *personal mastery. Lies and half-truths will always*
> *weigh you down, whereas truth will clear up your*
> *thinking and give you the energy and clarity*
> *needed for self-motivation.*

There are definitely rewards for integrity. In *The Book on Mind Management*, Dr. Dennis R. Deaton says, "Integrity is golden. Literally and figuratively more precious than rubies, we attain it as we seek it. Developing integrity, the portal to personal empowerment, happens incrementally, a step at a time. Yet the moment you make a strong commitment to strive for it, you acquire power! What counts most is your commitment to improve on this principle."

When we make a commitment to personal integrity, the Universe works in our favor. This was recognized by German philosopher Goethe when he said, "[The] moment one definitely commits oneself, then Providence moves, too. All sorts of things occur to help one that would never otherwise have occurred. A whole stream of events issues from the decision, raising in one's favor all manner of unforeseen incidents and meetings and material assistance, which no man could have dreamed could come his way."

The following exercise will help you to work on and increase your personal integrity:

1. Make a list of the ways that your life is currently "in integrity."

Pat yourself on the back, as you are on your way to success as you strengthen your personal integrity.

2. Make a list of the ways that you are not now "in integrity."

In addition to thinking about honesty, ask yourself the following questions:

- Do I do what I say I will do? (For example, if you tell someone that you will call him or her, do you make that call?)
- Do I meet my time commitments?
- Do I make promises that are impossible to keep?
- Do I say what I think people want to hear, rather than speaking the truth? (Consider that sometimes it is better to say nothing at all than to say something that is not true or to make an offensive comment.)
- Do I try to "look good" or cover up a mistake, rather than admitting the truth?
- Am I true to myself and who I am? Do I know who I am?
- Do I live my own values?

Ask yourself some of the following more specific questions:

- Am I working on the right degree program for me?
- Am I associating with people who are uplifting and positive?
- Do I live in fear or debt?
- Do I represent myself honestly?
- Do I put myself at undue physical risk?
- Do I take care of my health?
- Am I addicted to substances or compulsive behavior?

3. Analyze the source of each item on your list from number "2."

If these items are important to you, be sure to resolve all of them before moving to the next step. You might start by listing the consequences that result from each of them. Then write the changes you would need to make in order to eliminate the consequences and bring integrity to these parts of your life. It will help in your analysis if you also include anything that you may need to give up in order to bring these areas of your life into integrity.

4. Make a commitment to start living a life of integrity, as you define it.

Your integrity is unique to you, and you are the one who will decide what it means for you. You need to commit to commitment.

5. Let go of at least ten "shoulds," "coulds," "oughts," and "wills."

Many of us were conditioned as children to try to be everything to everyone. As we grew up, we learned that this is impossible; however, we continue to try to do this by telling ourselves that we *should* do this or that, or by making commitments that are impossible to keep.

6. Involve a coach or another strong person to help you.

Find an individual who is interested in partnering with you to help you to improve your personal integrity. This should be someone who truly cares about your well-being, wants the best for you, and is willing to tell you not only the things you want to hear. If you have a close friend, who is a positive person, you might consider doing this for each other.

7. Stop spending time with people who are not the best role models.

You know who these people are. Concentrate on spending your time with those people who are uplifting and from whom you receive the gift of positive energy.

8. Develop a realistic action plan for improving your personal integrity.

Keep this action plan simple. Include elements that you can actually do, rather than things that might occur. Once you have developed this plan, add it to your priority list, your goals, and your overall action plan that you developed earlier. Since personal integrity is a predecessor of success, I assume that it will be a priority for you if you want to create success in your life.

* * * * *

Personal integrity is a personal choice. Either you want it for your life, or you don't. However, the benefits of living in integrity are numerous. As you increase your level of integrity, you will begin to become aware of the following in your life:

- You will have more energy.
- You will feel almost effortlessness about achieving the results you want.
- You will feel much less stress in your life.
- You will attract into your life more fulfilling people who are consistently reliable, empowering, caring, and inspiring.
- You will enjoy a richer and more successful life.

In *Golden Nuggets*, Sir John Templeton says, "Probably the greatest secret to peace of mind is living the life of personal integrity—not what people think of you, but what you know of yourself. If you remain true to your ethical principles, your personal integrity can become an attractive beacon for success on every level. Listen carefully to the inner promptings of conscience and live peacefully."

Personal integrity is of utmost importance to success. It is your personal foundation on which you can build the person you want to be and continue to improve the wonderful person you see in the mirror each day.

Chapter Nine

Enjoy the Moment!

Create balance in your life

Adam is a wonderful planner. Each time I talk with him, he has had a "great brainstorm" for the next outing or social event. He plans trips to the football games, hiking adventures, talent competitions, and great parties. Everyone who participates in Adam's events tends to have a fantastic time. The only one who does not enjoy the events is Adam. His lack of enjoyment stems from the fact that he is continually focusing on planning the next event, rather than on the one that is occurring at the present time.

A physically attractive graduate student, Adam rarely dates the same woman more than once. He says that he would like to have a serious relationship and to be married while he is still in his twenties. He says he is looking for "Ms. Right" and even enlists some of his dates to help him look.

* * * * *

Stacey, who completed her degree in business management six years ago, is focused on her career. She is the first one to arrive in the office in the morning and the last one to leave in the evening, taking work home with her every night. She works at least seventy hours per week and has been promoted five times in six years. Her boss knows that he can depend on her to deliver results, even on very short notice.

Although Stacey enjoys her job, she wishes she had more time to do something other than work. She would like to visit her college roommate in another state, but she doesn't want to take the time away from work. In fact, she has not taken a vacation for several years. Her friends no longer invite her to their get-togethers, because they know that she will again tell them that she has to work. She is constantly tired and does not understand the reason for this. She thinks maybe she should see a doctor, but she is having difficulty scheduling this into her workload. She says, "I wish the doctor's office was open at 2:00 A.M. when I am having trouble sleeping."

Stacey tells herself that, after her next promotion, she will take time to do the things she wants to do. This is the same thing she had said before her last promotion and the one before that.

* * * * *

The stories of Adam and Stacey might look like extreme examples, but they are true. It is easy for a person to become absorbed in one part of his or her life and to be out of balance. We are meant to enjoy life. When we allow ourselves to be out of balance, we become more stressed. As a result, we enjoy life less. This limits our success.

Stopping to "smell the roses" is more than a cliché. It points out the importance of appreciating beauty, human relationships, and the things that are most important to us. It offers the opportunity to reflect, to decrease stress, and to add balance to our lives. This not only contributes to, but also enhances any success we may achieve.

When I received the job offer for my European assignment, my husband, Cliff, and I were excited about the opportunity ahead of us. I developed goals and objectives for the European job long before we left the United States. I wanted to make sure that my accomplishments were significant for the two years that I would be there and didn't give much thought to the wonderful adventures that would be available.

After I had been in Europe for two weeks, I sent status reports through electronic mail to those whom had been instrumental in helping me to receive the job offer. I will always cherish the answer that came from my United States human resource manager. He started by complimenting me on what I had already accomplished in the two weeks that I had been in Europe. He then added some advice by saying, "You will be given a lot of vacation time while you are on your European assignment. Be sure you take this time, and make it a point to see as much of Europe as you can. There are too many people who return from foreign assignments, never having taken advantage of the opportunity to explore the areas where they have lived. Many will remark, 'I worked so hard that I missed the party.' Enjoy the party while you are there."

I am grateful that this advice came very early during my European assignment. It allowed me to rethink my priorities and make the adjustments necessary to "enjoy the party" while still making the significant impact that I had planned. In fact, I think that the reason I was able to exceed my job objectives was due in part to the enjoyment of the adventures I experienced. Since Cliff was retired, he was able to travel with me on many of my business trips. I would plan meetings in London for Fridays and Mondays, so that we would be there for the weekend to spend time with friends, visit museums, and go to the theater. When we weren't in London or sightseeing in France, we would take short weekend trips to Germany, the Netherlands, and Belgium. We cruised the Mediterranean and Black Sea and took vacations to Italy, Spain, and Portugal. We also entertained many friends who visited us in France, and we enjoyed every minute of it. The added bonus was that I was able to exceed my objectives for the job assignment and to enjoy my job even more than I had anticipated.

Some of the graduates, who interviewed for this book, say that they have been accused of spending too much time working in order to reach the positions that they have held. However, this is not true. Although they focus on their careers, they also focus on their other priorities in life. They take time for themselves and for their families and friends. They truly enjoy life.

Dr. Bobbie Stevens, Unlimited Futures president, says, "It is so important to live in the *now*. The *now* is the one thing we can be sure of experiencing. Someone once said, 'Life is what happens when you are planning for your future.'"

Most of the graduates, who interviewed for this book, attended college full time immediately after high school. Carol Notto is an exception to this. She married within a year after graduating from high school, raised two beautiful daughters, and worked full time. She started working at 3M as a secretary and was promoted several times, even without a college degree. When 3M transferred her husband, Jeff, to Europe, Carol took a leave of absence from work, as it was impossible at that time for both she and Jeff to obtain work permits in Belgium. Carol had already passed her fortieth birthday when she decided to go back to school. While she and Jeff lived in Europe, Carol earned her bachelor's degree in business management from the University of Maryland and her master's degree in global marketing and communications from Emerson College. Upon returning to the United States at the end of Jeff's European assignment, 3M immediately promoted Carol to a management position in Corporate Marketing, giving her the opportunity to apply the things she had learned in college.

On the importance of taking time to enjoy your life, Carol says, "Balance in life is very difficult these days. Both my husband and I have had life-threatening illnesses. Because of these experiences, we've committed to a more balanced life, and we still find ourselves falling back into our 'working too much' habits from time to time. I think most people struggle with this. Of course there will be times when 'the job' will take over our lives, but most of us have some time frame as to when more normal hours will return. If we don't see that end in sight, then something is wrong. Having been seriously ill with breast cancer, I am thankful now for all things in life and appreciate them every day. I also do a lot more prioritizing, so I can enjoy the things that God wants me to do and feel some peace about that."

Admittedly, it is difficult for people who are focused on their careers to consciously take the time to "smell the roses." One person said, "I often feel that when I'm old and look back on my life, my main regret will be that I didn't enjoy the moment while I was living it. It won't be that I didn't achieve something, that I didn't make money, or that I didn't have the material things I wanted. I'm afraid that I won't feel that I have enjoyed it enough. My New Year's resolution this year was that, every time I went on a business trip, I was going to do one thing to have fun at my destination. It's hard to take the time to do it, but I'm doing it. There is something interesting to do on every business trip. I am taking the time, and I'm enjoying it."

Are you taking time to enjoy the moment and bring pleasure into your life? You might start by answering the following questions:

- Am I enjoying my college experience?
- Do I regularly take time for myself?
- Do I enjoy the company of special people?
- Do I enjoy the social events I attend?
- Do I live my priorities?
- Do I engage in recreational activities?
- Do I have at least one hobby?
- Do I take care of my health and have regular checkups?
- Do I exercise regularly?
- Do I give to others?
- Am I a gracious receiver?
- Do I have a way to relax that eliminates stress?

If you have answered "yes" to all of these questions, congratulations! Otherwise, the following suggestions may be of help:

I. Enjoy this time of your life.

The time that you are spending in college will be one of the most memorable times in your life. In forty years or so, when you are ready to retire from your career, you will still be talking about your college days. If life continues as it has been going since you started college, what will you be saying?

College is a hard work for most students, but it can also be a lot of fun. Are you having fun? Along with the long, tedious hours of studying, are you doing some things that you genuinely enjoy?

If you think you could be enjoying life more than you are right now, make a list of the things you would enjoy doing. When making this list, treat it as a brainstorming session with the following rules:

- Write down every idea for enjoyment that comes into your head.

- Don't judge these ideas as you are writing them down. (For example, don't think about whether you can afford to do these things.)

- When you think you have written all of your ideas, think of at least five more ideas for enjoyment.

- Review your list, crossing out anything that is illegal, immoral, or unethical.

- Considering current time and financial constraints, determine which things on your list are most feasible.

Now you can make plans to start doing some of the things on your list that are feasible. In addition to the education you are gaining, your college experience can be rewarding in so many ways.

2. Be in the present.

My department was responsible for developing a comprehensive strategic plan for 3M's e-Business, and top management had given us an extremely tight time line for delivering this plan. Several of the managers who reported to me worked long hours in order to meet the delivery schedule for the plan. At each critical point along the time line, we would meet to review progress and make any necessary modifications.

Late one Friday afternoon, one of the employees came to my office to ask when I would be leaving that day. She wanted to make sure that she gave me the latest draft of the plan to review that evening, so that I could get my recommendations back to her on Saturday morning. Her face was flushed from the intensity of the work that afternoon, and I was immediately concerned about her health. Mostly because of my concern for her, I explained that it was not necessary for her to get the draft to me that day. My husband and I had tickets for a professional football game that evening, and I would not have a chance to review the draft until Saturday morning. In her eagerness to meet the deadline, she replied, "I'll get it to you anyway." Half jokingly, she added, "So you can read it at the game!"

I brought the draft of the plan with me to the game and read it between plays. During plays, I thought about the future of e-Business and the things that my department needed to accomplish in order to be successful in this emerging channel. I definitely was not living in the present, and I was not taking the time to enjoy the game. In fact, I didn't even know the score throughout most of the game. In addition, I did not adequately review the plan document. In retrospect, I knew that it would have been much better for me to go to the game, enjoy the evening with my husband, and review the document the next morning when I could give it my full attention.

A colleague once said, "Being fully in the *present* is a *gift*. It is a gift to yourself as well as to others. You literally create your future with your thoughts and actions. When you are fully in the present, you are totally involved and alert to opportunities. The people you encounter subjectively sense whether or not you are fully with them. This has a great impact on the quality of your relationships."

3. Take time for yourself.

Many people will take the time to nurture others, but few will take the time to nurture themselves. Although they know it intellectually, they do not always accept the fact that they can best help others when they are physically, emotionally, mentally, and spiritually healthy.

In *Take Time for Your Life*, personal coach Cheryl Richardson suggests that her readers give themselves permission to make the quality of their lives their top priority. She stresses this in the following excerpt from her book:

> *A high-quality life starts with a high quality you. My basic coaching philosophy in working with clients is one of extreme self-care—the foundation of a rich and fulfilling life. This means putting your self-care above anything else— saying no unless it's absolute yes, choosing to spend your time and energy on things that bring you joy, and making decisions based on what you want instead of what others want. It's a challenging concept for most.*
>
> *Making your self-care a priority can be scary, even offensive, at first. Yet, as you begin to filter your decisions through the lens of extreme self-care, you'll find that your nagging inner voice becomes a strong ally in helping you to make better choices. You'll leave work early to keep that dinner engagement with a friend, or you'll go out for a walk during lunch instead of working straight through. And, best of all, you'll discover that when you start practicing extreme self-care, a Divine force rallies behind you to support your decisions and will actually make your life easier.*

Do you take time for yourself? When is the last time you went for a walk in the park and enjoyed nature? Engaged in a long phone conversation with a friend? Read a book that wasn't required for a class? Went to a movie or a play? If you had an entire day to do something spontaneous, what would it be? Why not do it this weekend?

4. Give to others.

Have you ever noticed how good you feel when you give to someone else? Some students wait to give until they can afford to buy an expensive gift. This is not necessary, as it is usually the nonmaterial gifts that the receiver values most. This can be as simple as a smile or a compliment. It can be the simple gift of showing someone that you care by giving him or her your attention. It can be taking the time to tell someone that you appreciate him or her. Although these gifts do not cost anything, they can be the most precious to both the receiver and the giver.

In the following passage from *The Seven Spiritual Laws of Success*, Dr. Deepak Chopra talks about giving:

> *When you meet someone, you can silently send them a blessing, wishing them happiness, joy, and laughter. This kind of silent giving is very powerful.*
>
> *One of the things I was taught as a child and, which I taught my children also, is never to go to anyone's house without bringing something— never visit anyone without bringing them a gift. You may say, "How can I give to others when at the moment I don't have enough myself?" You can bring a flower. One flower. You can bring a note or a card which says something about your feelings for the person you're visiting. You can bring a compliment. You can bring a prayer. Make a decision to give wherever you go, to whomever you see.*

5. Engage in recreational activities.

In *Your Money or Your Life*, Joe Dominguez and Vicki Robin note that the average North American has 32 percent less free time per week than their counterparts did in 1973. Even college students tend to rush through recreational activities, if they take the time to engage in them at all. However, it is these recreational activities that help to reduce stress and add to the fuel needed to accomplish your goals in life.

A recreational activity can be as simple as a walk outdoors. It can be a hobby, a visit with a friend, a sporting event, or a concert. It might be listening to music, dancing, or singing to yourself. Actually, it can be anything that you enjoy doing, including just taking time to relax.

The word *recreation* contains the root word *create*, which means, "to cause to exist." By preceding this word with the prefix *re*, which means "again" or "anew," we are saying that we are causing a new existence of ourselves. We are refreshing our lives, both mentally and physically.

Make a list of the ways that you are refreshing your life. From this list, you can determine whether you need to add some recreational activities that will help you to reduce stress and become renewed and refreshed. Your list from your earlier brainstorming session will help.

6. Express and feel gratitude.

Part of expressing gratitude is becoming a gracious receiver. Many people think that they should always be the giver, rather than the receiver; hence they have difficulty in accepting that which is given to them. Many have told me that they think they are not worthy or deserving.

You were born deserving of good things. If you do not remember this, look at a newborn baby. Is this baby deserving of love and happiness? You are no less deserving than you were on the day you were born. If you have doubt concerning your worthiness, look at your baby picture and remind yourself of this. When something good happens to you, tell yourself, "I deserve this." Be a gracious receiver, and express gratitude for that which you have been given.

Dr. Deepak Chopra suggests that we gratefully receive all the gifts that life has to offer us. These gifts include gifts of nature, such as sunlight, the sounds of singing birds, spring showers, and the beauty of the first snow of winter. They also include gifts from others, both material and nonmaterial.

* * * * *

In *Golden Nuggets*, Sir John Templeton says, "In order to be happy, healthy, and stress free, it is important to believe in yourself and your individual right to happiness and health. Take time to be out of doors. The beauty of the earth can stimulate joy, thanksgiving, and healthy thoughts. Learn to laugh and to be silent. . . . Life is to be lived and enjoyed!"

In these days of instant communication through the Internet, we have many opportunities that did not exist during our earlier years. While participating in a recent teleclass, I met Sara Arbel, an Israeli mother of three, who is a successful businesswoman. During our first class session, Sara and I discovered that, despite the cultural differences, we have much in common. We have communicated often through electronic mail since our first class together. Through these electronic mail messages, I have developed much respect for Sara and the decisions she has made in her life.

After her stint in the Israeli army, a responsibility required of all Israeli citizens, Sara married an aspiring artist. In the early years of her marriage, she pursued a higher education with course work in behavioral science, communication, and consumer psychology. She and her husband then moved to Canada, where she established an art gallery to market her husband's works of art. The customers kept returning, and she and her husband received large commissions. After nearly a decade, the couple and their children returned to their native Israel where Sara next established two businesses, one specializing in corporate image design and the other in marketing consulting. One business supplied work to the other, and they both became financially lucrative. She headed these companies as she was also raising her children. As the children got older, she traveled the world with her customers, who were from various industries, including electronics, plastics, agriculture, textile, medicine, and others. She competed well and was respected by her competitors. Her major challenges were during times of war when the entire economy was shaken. Still, she was extremely successful in business.

It seemed that Sara was living the ideal life—a good husband and family, a successful career, world travel, and financial security. Then her husband died, and her world fell apart. As a result, she threw herself even more into her career, working fourteen to sixteen hours each day.

Ultimately, Sara came to the realization that life was more than work alone and decided to work fewer hours and take time for her life. She is successful in her current profession as a consultant and a personal and professional coach. She is also successful in all other facets of her life.

When asked what advice she would give to students who want to achieve success in their lives, Sara said, "Don't forget yourself in the process of becoming successful. Forgetting yourself through this process is not a success in your life, but a success in only one aspect of your life. When you graduate, don't mistake between the making of a living and the making of a life, as the making of a life is the most valuable success story where you will leave a mark in the world. Invest first in yourself. . . . The rest will follow."

In *Tuesdays with Morrie*, Mitch Albom interviewed Morrie Schwartz, who was dying of amyotrophic lateral sclerosis, or what is more commonly known as Lou Gehrig's disease. Mitch asked Morrie what he would do if he had one perfectly healthy day. Morrie gave the following reply:

> *I would get up in the morning, do my*
> *exercises, have a lovely breakfast of sweet rolls*
> *and tea, go for a swim, then have my friends over*
> *for a nice lunch. I'd have them come one or two at a*
> *time so we could talk about their families, their*
> *issues, talk about how much we mean to each other.*
> *Then I'd go for a walk in a garden with some*
> *trees, watch their colors, watch the birds, take in*

the nature that I haven't seen in so long now.

In the evening, we'd all go together to a restaurant with some great pasta, maybe some duck—I love duck—and then we'd dance the rest of the night. I'd dance with all the wonderful dance partners out there, until I was exhausted. And then I'd go home and have a deep, wonderful sleep.

Mitch was surprised by Morrie's answer. He expected Morrie to say that, on his perfect day, he would fly to Italy or have lunch with the president. Instead, Morrie's answer was simple. It seemed average. During his illness, Morrie had much time to reflect on life and the things that brought him pleasure. It is sometimes the simplest things that bring us the most pleasure. I hope you will remember this lesson from Morrie ten years from now when you are entrenched in the career you will be seeking after college.

* * * * *

Often, when people are diagnosed with a terminal illness, they begin to think about what they would have done differently in their life. They think about their priorities and how they have lived them.

If you knew that you had just six more months to live and that you would have your health during this time, how would you live your life? What would you do differently? In contemplating these questions, I made a list of the things I would do:

- I would spend more time with my family and friends.
- I would be more spontaneous.
- I would show more emotions, laugh more, smile more, and cry more in front of other people.
- I would take better care of my body through exercise, sleep, and nutrition.
- I would not be concerned about what others think of me, but what I think of myself.
- I would record messages about life for my grandchildren.
- I would make myself more available to those in need and those less fortunate than I am.

- I would spend less time talking and more time listening.
- I would look for opportunities to engage in anonymous acts of kindness, even for people I do not know.
- I would open my eyes to the beauty of nature and enjoy witnessing the miracle of creation.
- I would express my love for other people, both in my words and in my actions.

After making this list, I decided that I didn't need to wait until I had just six months left of my life. I can do these things now.

Take time now to make your list. Then seize the joy of the day, savor each moment as special, and appreciate the wonder of life.

Chapter Ten

Continue to Learn!

Engage in a lifelong learning program after you graduate

When I finally graduated from college, I was thirty years old. Since I was a single mom and needed to work full time to support my family, most of my college education had been part time at night. Although excited that I had achieved a lifelong goal, I had no interest in engaging in any more education. A year later, I began realizing the importance of continuous learning, took the GMAT, and went back to school to earn my MBA.

Since you are in college, I assume that one of your major goals in life right now is to learn. Do you have any plans to continue in some type of a learning plan when you are finished with your degree program?

Just as my MBA degree opened doors for me before I had gained the experience needed for a particular position, education has been an important factor for many of those searching for expanded opportunities in the business world. Many of the graduates I interviewed have advanced degrees, and all of the interviewees are committed to lifelong learning.

Although learning might not seem like a top priority after you graduate, you will become more successful if you make time to continue your learning. Following are some of the options for incorporating learning into your life, both while you are in college and afterward:

1. Continue with your formal education.

You are doing this now and might consider additional degrees after you complete this one.

Nineteenth-century biologist Thomas Huxley said, "Perhaps the most valuable result of all education is the ability to make yourself do the thing you have to do when it ought to be done, whether you like it or not. It is the first lesson that [should] be learned and however early a person's training begins, it is probably the last lesson a person learns thoroughly."

2. Attend seminars and workshops.

Each day, thousands of seminars, workshops, and conferences are offered in various locations throughout the United States. Many of these are related to particular professions, and others provide personal growth and development. Some of them are free of charge, such as workshops offered by some church groups and nonprofit organizations.

Be selective when determining which seminars, workshops, and conferences to attend. Because of the number of these types of learning opportunities available, make sure that the ones you attend are the ones that will be the most beneficial, either professionally or personally.

Most people retain very little of what they learn in a seminar or workshop. For this reason, I recommend that you take notes, just as you are doing in your college classes now. Be sure to review these notes before much time has elapsed. During your review, develop an action plan on how you will apply what you have learned. If this action plan contains even one item that will be of benefit for you, it was worth the time you invested in attending the seminar.

Carol Notto, who earned both of her degrees while she was in her forties, said, "I can't say enough about the importance of continuing to learn. I am almost fifty-five years old, and every day is about learning. Stay open, positive, and excited to the concept of learning, because you will have to do it to stay current. A colleague of mine who recently decided to retire, said, 'I wish I could have taken all the classes that 3M had to offer. I didn't take the time to learn it all, because I didn't have the time, but at least I learned what I could. All that knowledge will help me in my next stage in life.'"

3. Read books, magazines, newspapers, and information available on the Internet.

A wealth of information on almost any subject is available in print and via the Internet. One of the great things about learning from these sources is that you can engage in this type of learning from almost anyplace, including in the comfort of your own home.

My advice in selecting reading material is the same as that for selecting conferences and workshops. Because of the quantity of books, magazines, and newspapers available, we need to be selective. This applies to the reading that we do for enjoyment, as well as the reading that we do in order to learn. It is unrealistic and counterproductive to attempt to read everything that comes into your home. Attempting to do so becomes overwhelming and can be a cause of neglecting priorities.

Read good books and other information. Determine which reading material is best for you by monitoring your attention span as you are reading, determining how much of the material you retain, and evaluating your feelings after reading the material. You will then improve your ability to select better reading material in the future.

4. Enhance your listening skills.

Listening to the spoken word is another way that we can learn. By listening to that which is happening around us, we learn so much more than we do when we are speaking. A child learns to stay away from danger by listening to his mother's warnings. A new mother or father learns to identify their baby's needs by listening to her different cries. Factory workers learn to perform their job responsibilities by listening to their foreperson's instructions. We all learn by listening to those who know more about a subject than we do.

In *The Art of Managing People*, authors Phillip L. Hunsaker and Anthony J. Alessandra offer the following tips for "power listening":

- Don't interrupt.
- Listen for main ideas.
- Concentrate on substance, not style.
- Fight distractions.
- Stifle anger.
- Take brief notes.
- Let others talk first.
- Empathize.
- Withhold judgment.
- React to the message.
- Read the feelings between the lines.
- Ask questions.

By spending more time listening and less time talking, we create learning opportunities that will increase our effectiveness and, ultimately, our success.

5. Listen to audiotapes.

We are living in a time of convenience with the many classes, seminars, and books that are available on audiotape and CD. If you have a tape or CD player in your car, you are able to make your driving time more productive by listening to tapes or CDs. If you cannot afford to buy audiotapes or CDs, you can check them out at the library or exchange tapes or CDs with others. Many companies also have libraries or human resource departments, which will lend learning tapes and CDs to employees.

If your only venue for listening to audiotapes or CDs is your car, it is advisable to listen to the tapes or CDs several times to maximize your learning opportunity. Some speakers recommend that you listen to a tape or CD five or six times. However, if you listen to a tape or CD for the first time while driving, you might want to also make time available to listen to it a second time when you can give it your full attention and take notes. You can then use these notes as you develop your learning plan.

6. Learn from life's experiences.

When my daughter was a teenager, I felt that I was constantly protecting and correcting her. When I realized that she resented this, I told her that I had made many mistakes in my life and that I would like to help her to learn from my mistakes. I thought that this would protect her from experiencing some of the pain I had felt as a result of these mistakes. Her answer surprised me when she said, "Mom, don't you think I will learn more from my own mistakes than I will learn from yours?" As much as I disliked the idea of my child experiencing pain, I realized she was right. We can learn from the experiences of others, but we learn even more from our own experiences, both positive and negative.

Successful people tend to be extremely aware of what is happening around them. They learn from both their own and other people's experiences. The things, which many people would call failures, are not failures to these people. They are learning opportunities. One of my interviewees failed her first test in graduate school. She said, "This showed me that I needed to work harder and to be more committed to what I was doing." She is convinced that her initial failure served as an inspiration to succeed.

An interviewee for one of my other books was terminated from one of her positions. She told me that this was a great learning opportunity, because it helped her to realize what she needed to do to improve her style. It also made her a stronger person. Since that time, she has excelled in every position she has held.

Each of us has hundreds of experiences from which we can learn each day. We learn through awareness, observation, and participation. Most of these learning opportunities have no financial cost to us, and they can provide substantial benefit to us.

In *Golden Nuggets*, Sir John Templeton says, "Wherever we are and whatever we are doing, it is possible to learn something that can enrich our lives and the lives of others. . . . No one's education is ever complete."

7. Challenge yourself with new experiences.

When Connie Carroll had been married for twenty-five years, she knew that she was a good wife, mother, grandmother, and home-maker. However, she wanted to increase her self-confidence, and she resolved to do this by overcoming her two major fears in life—speaking in public and swimming. To demonstrate her commitment, she entered the Mrs. Minnesota pageant as one of the few grand-mothers to compete in this competition.

Connie had a lifelong fear of water. Since she would be re-quired to model aerobic wear during the pageant, she engaged in an exercise program to become more physically fit and to lose some weight. She chose swimming as one of her main exercises and em-barked on a rigorous routine of lessons and practice. She swam three or four times each week. She not only lost weight and became more physically fit, but she also learned to be a good swimmer and over-came her fear of water.

Connie's next challenge was learning to be comfortable when speaking in public. This was a difficult one, as it is for most people. In fact, it is the number one fear of people in general. She knew that, during the pageant, she would be interviewed by judges and would also speak to the audience from the stage. She worked with a coach and then put what she learned into practice by extensive role-play-ing of mock interviews with family and friends. She became more comfortable speaking in public and eventually spoke not only at the pageant but also on television. "From this experience, I feel that I have become much more confident in myself and a more positive person" she told me. "I have learned that I have the ability to achieve the things I want. I have also learned how I can improve the way I communicate with others and the way I present myself."

Connie has since participated in three Mrs. Minnesota pag-eants, and she considers each of them a learning experience. She has enjoyed each pageant and has won awards for her community involvement and for having the best "pitch book." Her pitch book contains family pictures, certificates for volunteer work, diplomas, ribbons from dog shows, poems she had written, samples of her photography, and information on the ways she has represented her county. Preparing and using it enabled her to highlight areas in which she already had achieved a degree of success, and it was a great resource when she set out to solicit companies and individuals to sponsor her in the pageant.

Connie considers it a great honor to have been recognized for her community involvement. "This is an area that is so important to me and about which I feel so strongly. Being involved in organizations in your area shows you care about what is happening in your city, county, and schools. When you are aware, you can help to make positive changes."

Connie's community involvement has also provided learning experiences for her. Her volunteer activities in her school district, city, and state have helped more than thirty organizations. In her most recent volunteer activity, she is helping disabled people to ride horses. She explained, "Because of the motion of the horse, this program provides a therapeutic experience for disabled persons. It rhythmically moves the rider's body in a manner similar to a human walk. Physically disabled riders can show improvement in flexibility, balance, and muscle strength. The unique relationship formed with the horse can lead to increased confidence, patience, and self-esteem for people with mental or emotional disabilities."

Connie Carroll is a successful woman who has challenged herself and stepped out of her comfort zone in order to learn and to grow. Each of us has the opportunity to learn by challenging ourselves with new experiences. Start by making a list of areas in your life that you want to strengthen. From this, you can do some brainstorming regarding the things you might do in order to develop the strength you desire. Engaging in such a plan itself requires strength, but, as Connie has demonstrated, it is indeed achievable.

8. Work with a professional coach or mentor.

Looking back on my career, this far, the one thing I would do differently would be to engage a professional coach or mentor early in my career. If I had done so, I know I would have accelerated my success. Needless to say, I work with a professional mentor now.

There are thousands of professional coaches available to assist individuals in learning how to create success in their lives. According to Thomas Leonard, founder of Coach University, people hire coaches for the following reasons:

- To set better goals.
- To reach their goals faster.
- To make significant changes.
- To become more financially successful.
- To design—and live—the perfect life.
- To get ahead professionally.
- To make better decisions.
- To have someone with whom to collaborate.
- To improve their relationships.
- To make a bigger impact on the world.
- To simplify their life.
- To strengthen their personal foundation.
- To reduce stress and tolerations (unwanted things that they put up with).
- To increase income or revenues.
- To become a better manager, executive, or businessperson.

A coach or a mentor can be a valuable asset to you as you develop your learning plan and take action to create success in your life. If you don't have a coach or mentor now, I recommend that you find one as soon as you start your career after graduation.

9. Develop a personal learning plan.

Do you have a personal learning plan, aside from your degree curriculum? If not, you are not alone, as most people do not take the time to develop such plans. As a result, many people participate in learning activities that do not align with their top priorities and goals.

A personal learning plan need not be elaborate, nor does it need to take a long time to develop. Start by reviewing your priorities and goals and determining what it is that you need to know in order to achieve what you want in life. From there, you can decide the best methods for learning that which you need and/or want to know. By using the tips in this chapter, you can make a chronological list of your plans for acquiring the learning you want and need. It can be as simple as that.

Continuous, lifelong learning is important to success. Albert Einstein once said, "Education is that which remains when one has forgotten everything he learned in school." That which you learn throughout life contributes to your education and to your success.

Chapter Eleven

Increase Your Success!

Create an ideal life for yourself

What does success look like to you? For most students, this is a difficult question. We might point to another student and say that he or she is successful; however, we may be judging success by observing only one dimension of this student's life. In selecting interview candidates for this book, my first criterion was that the student or graduate needed to be successful in his or her own mind.

Most of the graduates I interviewed are businesspersons. Although they all have attained success in their careers, they agree that a successful career is not the only component of a successful life. They are confident that they would be successful in any career they might have chosen and are happy with who they are and what they're doing. You can determine what success means to you personally. Right now, it might mean good grades, graduating from college, a certain type of recognition, or excelling in sports or other extracurricular activities. Later, it might include a well-paying career, an emotionally or spiritually rewarding job, and/or financial security, as well as a wonderful family. The bottom line is that only *you* can define your own success.

How do you personally define success? If you could create the ideal life for yourself, what would that be? If you don't have your own definition, it might help to review the definitions given by some of the interviewees in the introduction:

- *Success is being able to look at the person in the mirror every morning and feel good that you are achieving what you set out to achieve and done so in an honorable way.*

- *Success is a feeling of continually moving forward but the ability to be happy standing still.*

- *Success is positive contribution to self, society, and the environment.*

- *Success is feeling happy each day.*

- *Success is a feeling of accomplishment and fulfillment.*

- *Success is the achievement of goals that are important to you.*

- *Success is living comfortably with who you are and what you have.*

- *Success is not only having a fulfilling career where I know I am making a difference, but it's also having time to pursue outside interests.*

- *Success is having peace of mind, free from unnecessary concern over the future and being able to dwell in the now moment.*

- *Success is when both my work and my personal life are fulfilling.*

- *Success is a balance in personal and professional life.*

- *Success is being known as a person with values and integrity.*

- *Success is a mental, physical, emotional, and spiritual balance in one's life.*

- *Success is enjoying each day.*

- *Business success is achieving a position in a profession the individual enjoys.*

- *Success is maintaining personally acceptable levels of progress toward identifiable personal goals.*

- *If I can positively touch one person, plant a seed, or do a good act, each day, then that day is successful.*
- *Success is the quiet peace of knowing I did my absolute best.*
- *Success is achieving one's full potential.*

Once you have defined what success means to you, you are in a position to achieve that success. If you have completed the exercises in this book, you are on the road to increasing your success. You first need to believe in yourself.

When I was fourteen years old, my goal was to be a computer programmer, even though this was not a common field for women at that time. I believed that I could do this. Although I took some detours along the way, I became a computer programmer. Later, after I had designed computer systems for marketing and sales, I decided that I wanted to combine my computer experience with marketing to enhance the effectiveness of marketing and sales. This led to the management of functions that did not exist before I became involved in them. All along, I knew that I could do it. And I did!

Once you have defined what success looks like for you, the next step is to visualize that success. Remember to visualize the result of this success as if it has already happened.

Be aware of your priorities in life, and set your goals and act according to these priorities. Be sure that your priorities are aligned with your values and your definition of success. The more you act according to your priorities, the more likely it will be that you will enjoy success.

Take time to focus on those things that are most important to you. You may need to practice the focusing exercises in order to increase your ability to focus.

Evaluate your attitude each day, and stay away from the three C's—complaining, criticizing, and condemning. The more positive your attitude, the more you will attract that which is positive into your life.

Personal integrity is tantamount to success. Before making a commitment, be sure that you will keep it. Let your word be your bond.

Create balance in your life. Take time to be spontaneous and to have fun. We are meant to enjoy life.

Even after you graduate from college, take advantage of every opportunity to learn. Before going to bed each night, think about the things that you have learned that day and the ways that you will apply these things in creating your ideal life and in enriching the lives of others.

> *A successful life involves personal relationships, family experiences, and spiritual involvement, as well as our professional lives. There may be many life possibilities for each of us. Success is finding out which of these may be the most meaningful, working hard for these dreams, and giving credit for the help and guidance necessary to fulfill them.*
>
> —Sir John Templeton

By integrating and incorporating the ten success strategies into your life, you will increase your potential for enjoying the success that you seek. The ten success strategies really work! They have worked for me, for the book interviewees, and for the people I have coached and mentored. They will work for you, too.

I wish you success!

Appendix A

Advice to Students

From Successful Graduates

At the end of each of my interviews, I asked the college graduates to share some advice with students on how to be successful. The preceding chapters include some of this advice. Additional advice from several of the interviewees is included in this appendix.

From K. D. Taylor, associate dean at Utah Valley State College, graduate of Brigham Young University:

> 1. *Set goals. Know what it is you want to accomplish at the start. Then plan how to accomplish it. If the task seems too big, break it down into a series of smaller goals that seem more manageable.*
>
> 2. *Be open to alternative or creative options. It's okay to change your mind about your goals.*
>
> 3. *When the setbacks occur, keep moving forward. Don't let temporary delays or frustrations deter you. Realize that you are human and will have failures. That's okay as long as you don't let the failure be the end of your effort.*
>
> 4. *Enjoy the journey. Find ways to make the learning interesting to you. Celebrate the acquisition of new ideas.*

> 5. *Maintain a high level of integrity. Nothing is more important than being true to yourself.*
>
> 6. *Have faith in your own abilities. Believe that you can do whatever you truly want to, but don't be reluctant to ask for help from sources greater than yourself.*
>
> 7. *Be competitive when necessary, but be compassionate always. Encourage those around you to experience their own victories, facilitating and celebrating their successes with them whenever possible.*

From Jeff Notto, international business development manager, graduate of St. Thomas University:

> *Know who you are, be yourself, and don't compromise your integrity. Don't compromise who you are in order to get to where you think you should be. If you continue to develop your skills (both your interpersonal skills and your professional skills), given a little time, you will realize your goals.*

From Nicholas Kahler, Army field artillery officer, graduate of United States Military Academy at West Point:

> 1. *Learn to deal will ALL types of people in every situation.*
>
> 2. *Develop a strong, efficient work ethic.*
>
> 3. *Balance work and play.*
>
> 4. *Learn to recognize excuses, and don't make them.*

From Rebecca O'Neill, attorney, graduate of University of Florida:

> *Find your divine path and follow it. You will be successful if you find that one thing that makes you happy. Personal fulfillment is more important than money. However, these are not mutually exclusive. If you are in a profession that gives you joy, you will have enough. If you love what you do, you will be successful by virtue of deriving great pleasure in your work.*

From Carol Notto, business process manager, graduate of University of Maryland and Emerson College:

> *The work ethic and high standard of commitment that you learn to use in college will stay with you when you go on to the working world. To some today, it may sound old-fashioned, but it's not. A strong work ethic that includes doing what you commit to doing, showing up on time, and turning in your best effort in school also, for the most part, sums up a lot of what it takes to get ahead in the workplace. I've found out that there really are no shortcuts to success when it comes to a high work ethic. Be honest, because dishonesty will catch up with you sooner or later. Be honest with your commitment to completing tasks, and give credit where credit is due. Your colleagues will appreciate that and see that you are a team player—not just out to make yourself "shine" in the eyes of the boss.*
>
> *Try to find excitement in what you're doing, even if it's not your "dream" class or your "dream" job. Believe in the high level goals of the project, organization, or whatever it is you're working on, even if your assignment is what you might consider beneath you. I have a poster in my office at 3M that says, "Every day, 3M people find new ways to make amazing things happen. The company's customers know they can rely on 3M to help make their lives better." I truly believe that my job at 3M is not just a job. It's a way to make the world better, and I'm a part of that.*

From Dan Love, retired business strategist, aviation industry, graduate of Stanford University:

> *Be passionate about whatever it is you do, or
> don't do it. This presupposes choosing what you
> do, planning how to achieve what you want, and a
> willingness to change directions when things do
> not turn out as you desire.*

From Becky Creighton, real estate investor, graduate of Ohio State University:

- *Get a job while in college that is related to your field of interest for your career.*
- *Get to know your professors, as they are a wealth of knowledge, literally and for the people they know.*
- *Be persistent! I was turned down from OSU and received my degree from there. I was turned down by AT&T for a sales job, and I worked for them for seven years (three of which I was one of their top sales representatives). My husband broke up with me in 1988 while we were dating, and, in 1993, we were married. Be persistent!*
- *Network! Network! Network! If you don't know how, join a networking organization.*

From Keith Geilman, sales manager, graduate of Utah State University:

> *Define what you want. Decide what you are
> willing to pay for it in time, effort, family and
> delayed gratification, and then work to that end.
> Remember that no company will ever be as loyal
> to you as your family, so be careful not to offer
> them (your family) upon the altar of sacrifice that
> is needed to attain worthwhile goals or, in other
> words, success.*

From Stephanie Kane, business planning associate, graduate of University of Dayton, Ohio:

> *Be patient. Take time in discovering what it is
> you want to do. Don't let your entire life be*

*identified with the first or second job you have
out of college, because you're going to want to
do that. In college, you're accustomed to saying
"I'm a marketing major," or "I'm a golfer," and
you have identified with that goal as who you
are. Just because you are a sales associate, it
doesn't mean it's "who" you are. It's "what you
do." It might not be gratifying, but don't believe
you are trapped in that job for the rest of your
life. You will learn something from the experience
and the people you meet through it. It will help
you in the next job or role you take. Take it one
day at a time, take action, and be aggressive.
Don't be discouraged. The first two years after
college are a HUGE time of transition, and you
will do well if you are prepared for it.*

From Jill Lublin, international professional speaker, radio and television host, best-selling author and public relations consultant, graduate of Wayne State University:

- *Start early to be a learner, and not just a college learner. Enroll in personal growth-oriented workshops and activities.*

- *Engage in some financial education. I wish I had learned to read a profit and loss statement and perform a cash flow analysis while I was in college.*

- *Set goals for the things you want to create and accomplish in your life. Mark Victor Hansen says to make a list of 100 life goals, and, when you have accomplished all of them, make a new list of 100 more goals. Having a list of three powerful goals for right now is a good way to start.*

- *Dream bigger than what you think you can accomplish.*

From Marcy Swan, trainer of foster parents and shelter care provider, graduate of Brigham Young University:

> *Learn for the sake of knowledge gained.*
> *College is not a race to finish first. Don't take*
> *shortcuts. Keep your life's priorities in mind.*

From Annie O'Connor, corporate director, Musculoskeletal Practice at Rehabilitation Institute of Chicago, graduate of St. Louis University at Northwestern University:

> *Perseverance—Do not take no for an answer.*
> *Patience—Enjoy the process.*
> *Passion—Pursue your interest.*

From Jim Paschal, engineer and aircraft designer, graduate of Arizona State University:

- *Recognize that the greatest knowledge of life cannot always be obtained from academia. My truth about life is far grander now than could ever be taught in college. Open your mind and embrace the vast knowledge that exists in the nooks and crannies of society. I find that great realizations about the universe often come from obscure places that you would never expect to look in.*

- *Get over the notion that you are as good as you will ever be. You have no idea of the powerful and capable being you can evolve into. For instance, we are all taught that IQ can never improve, when in fact I boosted mine over thirty points while doing my personal advancement work. Self-improvement is the only real way you will ever move to far greater levels of success, because the only element that really holds you back in this world is you. The old saying goes that if you do the things you've always done, then you will continue to get the things you've always gotten.*

- *Never give up in the pursuit of your dreams and goals. The only real failures are those who quit. Virtually all successful people, including myself, failed many times along the way, but, in the end, it never mattered how many battles were lost, only whether or not they won the war. And no one will remember anything about your war but your final outcome, so make it a victory!*

From Marilyn Straka, author, founder of tour business, graduate of Macalester College:

> *1. Study hard, but have fun, too. Have a good balance.*
> *2. Meet people and develop a network that will be helpful throughout life.*

From Dr. Nathan Wood, licensed marriage and family therapist, graduate of Brigham Young University:

- *Define your value/priority list, and live by it. I would make sure relationships with friends or family come on top of the list, however. No amount of money or academic success can buy happy relationships.*

- *Define success for yourself. Use yourself as your own best measuring stick of progress. There will always be someone smarter, better, or faster than you.*

- *Above all, enjoy the journey. That way, you won't be disappointed when you reach your destination.*

From Dr. Michael Norwood, author and chiropractor, graduate of Life Chiropractic College:

> *Go with your passion. If you have a love in life, don't make it secondary to earning money. For example, if you passionately love sports, and there's nothing else you want to do, then find a career in sports. Even if you don't have the talent to play professional sports, you might get a job as an announcer, sports writer, or broadcaster. To be truly successful in a field, you have to get past all of the obstacles, and it's much easier when you love what you're doing.*

Appendix B

Reference Guide

To Creating Success in Your Life

Individual Definitions/Components of Success

- Being able to look at the person in the mirror every morning and feel good that you are achieving what you set out to achieve and done so in an honorable way
- A feeling of continually moving forward but the ability to be happy standing still
- Positive contribution to self, society, and the environment
- Feeling happy each day
- A feeling of accomplishment and fulfillment
- Achievement of goals that are important to you
- Living comfortably with who you are and what you have
- Having a fulfilling career where you know you are making a difference, while also having time to pursue outside interests
- Peace of mind, free from unnecessary concern over the future and being able to dwell in the now moment
- When both work and personal life are fulfilling
- Balance in personal and professional life
- Being known as a person with values and integrity

- Mental, physical, emotional, and spiritual balance in one's life
- Enjoyment of each day
- Achievement of a position in a profession the individual enjoys
- Maintaining personally acceptable levels of progress toward identifiable personal goals
- Positively touching one person, planting a seed, or doing a good act, each day
- The quiet peace of knowing you did your absolute best.
- Achievement of one's full potential.
- Whatever you define success to be for you

Strategies for Success

- Believe in Yourself!
- Dare to Dream!
- Determine Your Priorities!
- Set Powerful Goals!
- Ready—Aim—Take Action!
- Stay Focused!
- Remain Positive, No Matter What!
- Live your Life with Integrity!
- Enjoy the Moment!
- Continue to Learn!

Ways to Increase Self-esteem

- Think of yourself as the important person you are.
- Practice daily personal affirmations.
- Emulate self-confident people.
- Reward yourself for each success.
- Surround yourself with positive people.
- Look and feel your best.
- Fake it until you make it.
- Affirm those around you.

Relaxation Process

1. Sit down, close your eyes, and let the chair support your body.
2. Uncross your legs and feel yourself sink into the chair.
3. Take a deep breath, inhaling slowly. Hold your breath. Then slowly exhale as you imagine the tension leaving

your body. Repeat this four times, each time becoming more aware of your breathing.

4. Let all your muscles relax as much as you can before going through the following steps.

5. Tense the muscles of your feet and ankles, curling your toes. Gently release this tension until your feet and ankles are totally relaxed.

6. Tense the muscles in the lower part of your legs. Slowly release this tension.

7. Tense the muscles in your upper-legs. As before, slowly release the tension from your legs. Your legs, ankles, and feet should now be fully relaxed and feel like they are hanging limply.

8. Tense your hips and abdomen. As before, let this area of your body relax slowly.

9. Tense your chest and back muscles. Slowly, gently relax these muscles.

10. Direct your attention to your hands. Quickly make two fists, and slowly relax your hands.

11. Bend your wrists. Then relax them.

12. Tense the muscles in your lower arms. Slowly let them relax. Do the same with your upper arms.

13. Shrug your shoulders. Let them relax. Shrug them a second time, and then let them relax even more. Your arms are now beginning to hang comfortably by your sides.

14. Turn your head from side to side as far as it will go. Do this again. Touch your chin to your chest, and then raise it as high as you can. Relax your neck muscles.

15. Clench your teeth tightly together. Now relax your jaw muscles. Smile as broadly as you can. Then relax your mouth. Wrinkle your nose. Relax it. Close your eyes tighter. Relax them. Wrinkle your forehead. Relax it, feeling the tension flow out of your head.

16. If there still are any tense muscles in your body, direct your attention to these muscles. Relax them one-by-one.

Visualization Process

1. Determine what you want to create in your life.
2. Eliminate distractions.
3. Relax your body and your mind.
4. Create a mental movie.
5. Reinforce your vision through consistent mental rehearsal.

Steps to Setting Priorities

1. Determine your true values.
2. Prioritize your value list.
3. Plan and prioritize your activities.
4. Make time for your highest priorities.

Setting Powerful Goals

- Commit your goals to paper.
- Assure that your goals are realistic and achievable, but give them some "stretch" to allow room for growth.
- Clearly define your goals.
- Visualize your goals as if you have already achieved them.
- Describe the benefits of your goals.
- Commit to accomplishing your goals.
- Develop and implement an action plan.

Additional Goal-setting Tips

- Identify your major obstacles to goal achievement.
- Set a deadline and a schedule for accomplishment.
- Reward yourself as you reach milestones on the way to accomplishing your goal.
- Review your goals every morning and every evening.
- Be clear about what you want to accomplish.

Decision Analysis Process

1. On a piece of paper, draw a chart showing the alternative decisions across the top and the decision-making criteria along the left side. Under each alternative, leave room for two columns that will be used later in this analysis. This chart can also be done on a computer spreadsheet (see Appendix C).
2. For each criterion, assign a weight between 1 and 5, and

write this weight next to the criterion.

3. Evaluate each alternative for each criterion by assigning a score between 0 and 5, with "5" meaning the alternative very highly meets the criterion and "0" meaning that the alternative does not at all meet the criterion. Write the score in the cell (the box at the cross-section of the alternative and the criterion).

4. Multiply the weight of the criterion by the score of the criterion for each alternative. Write this number in a separate column under each alternative.

5. Add the weighted scores for each alternative.

6. Compare the totals. (If one of the totals is significantly higher than the others, this is the alternative that best meets the criteria. If there is not a significant difference between the highest total and the second highest total, you can either make a judgment call or add more criteria.)

Problem-solving Process

1. Write a synopsis of the current situation, clearly describing the problem. Be as objective as possible.

2. Determine the root cause of the problem. This might start with a list of probable causes. Take into consideration that the problem may be a symptom of another problem and that there can be more than one root cause.

3. Evaluate the root cause to determine what can be changed.

4. Brainstorm alternative solutions for solving the problem.

5. Evaluate each of the alternative solutions.

6. Select and implement the best alternative.

Handling Distractions

1. Set aside quiet time during the day to focus on your top priorities or action steps.

2. Decrease the stress in your body and your mind through relaxation.

3. Keep a piece of paper and a pen at hand while you are concentrating on a project or task. When an unrelated thought enters your mind, write it down.

4. Continue to record your distractions and the methods that you use to deal with them. Note the progress you are making in this area.

Methods for Improving Attitude

- Refrain from complaining, criticizing and condemning.
- Eliminate worry from your life.
- Put on a happy face.
- Look for the good in everything.
- Know that you can do it.
- Laugh.
- Value other people.
- Set an example.
- Give back to society.

Method for Improving Integrity

1. Make a list of the ways that your life is currently "in integrity."
2. Make a list of the ways that you are not now "in integrity."
3. Analyze the source of each item on your list from number "2."
4. Make a commitment to start living a life of integrity, as you define it.
5. Let go of at least ten "shoulds," "coulds," "oughts," and "wills."
6. Involve a coach or another strong person to help you.
7. Stop spending time with people who are not the best role models.
8. Develop a realistic action plan for improving your personal integrity.

Ways to Create Balance and Enjoy Life

- Enjoy this time of your life.
- Be in the present.
- Take time for yourself.
- Give to others.
- Engage in recreational activities.
- Express and feel gratitude.

Options for Learning

- Continue with your formal education.
- Attend seminars and workshops.
- Read books, magazines, newspapers, and information available on the Internet.
- Enhance your listening skills.
- Listen to audiotapes.
- Learn from life's experiences.
- Challenge yourself with new experiences.
- Work with a professional coach or mentor.
- Develop a personal learning plan.

Appendix C

Decision Analysis Chart

Criteria	Weight	Alternatives							
		Alternative 1		Alternative 2		Alternative 3		Alternative 4	
		Score	Weight x Score	Score	Weight x Score	Score	Weight x Score	Score	Weight x Score
Totals									

Appendix D

Recommended Reading

Albom, Mitch. *Tuesdays with Morrie*. New York, N.Y.: Doubleday, 1997.

Benton, Debra A. *Lions Don't Need to Roar*. New York, N.Y.: Warner Books, 1994.

Chandler, Steve. *100 Ways to Motivate Yourself*. Franklin Lakes, N.J.: Career Press, 1996.

Chandler, Steve. *Reinventing Yourself*. Franklin Lakes, N.J.: Career Press, 1998.

Covey, Stephen R. *The 7 Habits of Highly Effective People*. New York, N.Y.: Simon & Schuster, 1990.

Deaton, Dennis R. *The Book on Mind Management*. Mesa, Ariz.: MMI Publishing, 1994.

Dyer, Wayne W. *You'll See It When You Believe It*. New York, N.Y.: Avon Books, 1990.

Frishman, Rick and Lublin, Jill. *Networking Magic*. Avon, Mass.: Adams Media, 2004.

Gustafson, Joan, et. al. *Success Is a Decision of the Mind*. Sevierville, Tenn.: Insight Publishing, 2004.

Malinchak, James. *From College to the Real World*. Coral Springs, Fla.: Positive Publishing, 1998.

Maltz, Maxwell. *Psycho-Cybernetics*. New York, N.Y.: Pocketbooks, 1987.

Norwood, Michael. *Taking Stock: A Soul's Journey through Life, Death and the World of Investment*. Sedona, Ariz.: Global Publishing, 1997.

Norwood, Michael. *The Making of the Wealthy Soul*. Sedona, Ariz.: Global Publishing, 2001.

Norwood, Michael. *The Vision of the Wealthy Soul*. Sedona, Ariz.: Global Publishing, 2001.

Peale, Norman Vincent. *The Power of Positive Thinking*. Englewood Cliffs, N.J.: Prentice-Hall, Inc., 1978.

Richardson, Cheryl. *Take Time for Your Life*. New York, N.Y.: Broadway Books, 1999.

Stevens, Bobbie. *Unlimited Futures: How to Understand the Life You Have and Create the Life You Want*. Naples, Fla.: Tara Publishing, 2001.

Templeton, Sir John. *Golden Nuggets*. Radnor, Pa.: Templeton Foundation Press, 1997.

vos Savant, Marilyn. *Brain Building*. New York, N.Y.: Bantam Doubleday Dell Publishing, 1991.

Index

3M
accepting offer with, 109
new position at, 41–42, 60
working for, 37, 45, 81–82, 137, 141, 156, 158–59, 183
7 Habits of Highly Effective People, The, 67
100 Ways to Motivate Yourself, 147
101 Ways to Make Every Second Count, 75

A
action lists, 73–75. *See also* checklists
action plan
for achieving goals, 39, 51, 92–95, 179
examples of, 101–5
for job offers, 107–9
for personal integrity, 150
for success, 101–12
action, taking, 97–112
Activision, 82
advice for students, 181–87
affirmations, 30–32, 38
Albom, Mitch, 164
Alessandra, Anthony J., 170
alignment in life, 146–47. *See also* balance in life
Allen, Steve, 49
Arbel, Sara, 163–64
Aristotle, 50
Arizona State University, 100, 115, 180
Art Institute of Phoenix, 29

Art of Managing People, The, 170
attention spans, 113–14, 116
attitudes, altering, 125–38, 179, 194
audiotapes, 170–71

B
balance in life, 76–77, 146–47, 153–66, 180–82, 187, 194–95
belief in self, 25–26, 29, 35, 38–39, 179, 182
Bell, Alexander Graham, 85
benefit statement, 90–91
Bly, Robert W., 75
Book on Mind Management, The, 43, 57, 148
Bowersock, Terri, 86
Boyfriend, The, 24
Brain Building, 30, 119
brainstorming, 93–94, 158, 173
Branden, Nathaniel, 147
Brigham Young University, 26, 29, 181, 185, 187

C
Camelot, 24
Carnegie, Dale, 127
Carroll, Connie, 172
Carroll, Lewis, 80
CDs, 170–71
challenges, 25, 94–95, 123–24, 172–73, 187
Chandler, Steve, 147
checklists, 63, 67, 73–75, 78
Chicken Soup for the Soul series, 58
Chopra, Deepak, 161, 163
Cisco Systems, 25
Civil Service Department, 27–28
clarity, 84, 148
Coach University, 146, 174
coaches, 150, 164, 173–74
commitment
  to challenges, 172–73
  to goals, 92, 106
  to lifelong learning, 167–75
  to personal integrity, 143, 146–50, 180
  to priorities, 65, 70, 77
  commitment statement, 90, 92
complaints, 127–28, 179

concentration, 113–21
condemnation, 127–28, 179
conferences, 168
confidence, 38. *See also* self-confidence
conscious mind, 30, 57–58
continuous learning, 167–75, 180, 186, 195
contributions, 69–70, 75–76, 138, 161
Control Theory, 56
Covey, Stephen, 67, 73
Crandell, Lois, 50, 52, 56
Creighton, Becky, 28, 87, 99, 144, 184
criticisms, 127–28, 179
Crowell, Gayle, 69–71, 138, 144

D
da Vinci, Leonardo, 93
daily action list, 73–75. *See also* checklists
daily affirmations, 30–32, 38
Dallas Cowboys, 121
Danforth, William H., 138
David, 59–60
de Chardin, Teilhard, 85
Deaton, Dennis, 30, 41, 56–57, 59, 90, 148
decision analysis, 103, 106–9, 192–93, 197
desires, 41, 52–53, 60, 82–84
destiny, 30, 41
Disney, Walt, 48
distractions, 53–54, 113–17, 193–94
Do the Dream, 48
Dominguez, Joe, 162
Dow Corning, 115, 136
dreams, 24–25, 48, 52–57, 61, 95. *See also* visualizations
Drucker, Peter, 137
Dyer, Wayne, 49

E
Edison, Thomas, 99
educational goals, 88, 167–75, 180, 186, 195
Einstein, Albert, 45, 175
Eisenhower, Dwight, 66
Elnadry, Jeanne, 116, 134, 144
Emerson College, 183
Emerson, Ralph Waldo, 58, 138

energy
    mental energy, 43, 45, 148, 151
    negative energy, 123, 127–28
    physical energy, 43, 45, 148, 151
    positive energy, 123, 128, 150
enjoying life, 76–77, 146–47, 153–66, 180–82, 187, 194–95
Entrepreneur Magazine, 86

F
failure
    consequence of, 110
    experiences with, 124–25
    fear of, 109–10
    overcoming, 186–87
    probability of, 110
family priorities, 64, 70, 72, 77, 99, 180, 184, 187
fears
    of failure, 109–10
    overcoming, 36–37, 172–73
    of rejection, 29
focus
    on goals, 121, 179
    importance of, 113–21
    keys to, 117–19
    on priorities, 115–16, 120–21, 156–57, 179
    forgiveness, 131–32
Foster, Judy, 58
Freud, Sigmund, 97

G
Geilman, Keith, 94, 99, 144, 184
General Mills, 76
Gerrish, Christina, 29, 51
"giving back," 138
Glasser, William, 56, 57
goals
    achieving, 79–86, 92–95
    action plan for, 39, 51, 92–95, 179
    and affirmations, 32
    benefits of, 90–91
    brainstorming, 93–94
    commitment to, 92, 106
    defining, 80, 87–89, 95, 184

determining, 52–53
   focus on, 121, 179
   setting, 80–81, 84–95, 181–82, 185, 192
   visualizing, 52–57, 83, 89–90
   written goals, 84–85, 95
Goethe, 67, 148
Golden Nuggets, 131, 151, 163, 171
GoodNews Media, 121
GoodNews TV, 48
gratitude, 162–63
Grinding It Out: The Making of McDonald's, 50
Guerrilla Publicity, 35, 48
Gustafson, Cliff, 42, 44–47, 91–92, 128, 154–55

H
Hamilton, Alexander, 115
Hansen, Mark Victor, 58, 185
happiness, 30, 43, 51, 129–30, 162–63
healing power, 135–36
helping others, 136–38, 161
Hill, Napoleon, 32, 58, 90
Hilton, Conrad, 50
honesty, 36–37, 145–46, 149, 183
Hope, Bob, 136
Hosseinioun, Mishana, 76
Houston, Jean, 58
Hugo, Victor, 73
Hunsaker, Phillip L., 170
Huxley, Thomas, 168

I
I Dare You!, 138
ideal life, 41, 43, 177–80
images, 55–57, 89. *See also* visualizations
Inc. magazine, 86
integrity, 36, 141–51, 180, 182, 194
Intuitive Manager, The, 30

J
James, William, 125
job offers, 107–9
Johnson, Jimmy, 121
Jolley, Willie, 110

K

Kahler, Nicholas, 78, 99, 134, 182
Kane, Stephanie, 76, 100, 121, 184
Killey, Jean Claude, 110
Kroc, Ray, 50

L

laughter, 135–36
Law of Success, The, 90
learning goals, 88, 167–75, 180, 186, 195
Leonard, Thomas J., 146, 174
lies, 141–42, 148
life balance, 76–77, 146–47, 153–66, 180–82, 187, 194–95
Life Chiropractic College, 23, 187
life, enjoying, 76–77, 146–47, 153–66, 180–82, 187, 194–95
life experiences, 171–72
life management, 66, 71, 160–61
lifelong learning, 167–75, 180, 186, 195
Lincoln, Abraham, 97
listening skills, 169–70
Louisiana State University, 25
Love, Dan, 142, 183
Lublin, Jill, 35, 48, 120, 185

M

Macalester College, 105, 187
Macy, R. H., 110
Maltz, Maxwell, 58
manifestations, 43–53, 60, 84. *See also* visualizations
McDonald's, 50
Mental Athlete, The, 58
mental energy, 43, 45, 148, 151
mental exercise, 119
mental images, 50, 55–57. *See also* visualizations
mental rehearsal, 57
mentors, 47, 173–74. *See also* personal coaches
Merv Griffin Show, 50
Michelangelo Principle, 59–60
mind, strengthening, 30–31, 117–18. *See also* conscious mind;
subconscious mind
    mission statement, 71
    moment, living in, 153–66
    motivation, 87, 144, 147–48

N
negative chemical reactions, 134
negative comments, 30
negative conversations, 35
negative energy, 123, 127–28
networking, 35, 92, 184, 187
Networking Magic, 35, 48
New York Times, 49
Nicklaus, Jack, 97–98
Nightingale, Earl, 30, 51
Northwestern University, 133, 186
Norwood, Michael, 23–26, 50, 115, 133, 187
Notto, Carol, 156, 168, 183
Notto, Jeff, 80–82, 137–38, 182

O
obstacles, 25, 94–95, 123–24, 172–73, 187
O'Connor, Annie, 133, 186
Ohio State University, 28, 99, 184
Once upon a Mattress, 24
O'Neill, Rebecca, 29, 99–100, 144, 182
Oprah Winfrey Show, 50, 86
Oracle Corporation, 25
organizational skills, 67, 70, 100

P
Paine, Thomas, 93
Paschal, Jim, 100, 115, 186
passion, 184, 186–87
Patanjali, 90
patience, 184, 186
peace, 147, 151, 157
Peale, Norman Vincent, 124
Penn, William, 136
perseverance, 100, 186
persistence, 184
personal coaches, 150, 164, 173–74
personal integrity, 36, 141–51, 180, 182, 194
personal learning plan, 174–75. *See also* lifelong learning
personal mission statement, 71
physical energy, 43, 45, 148, 151
physical exercise, 119
physical limitations, 86

Portable Coach, The, 146
Porter, Kay, 58
Portinga, Dean, 43–45, 55, 127, 132
positive affirmations, 30–32, 38
positive attitude, 133–34, 138–39, 179–80
positive chemical reactions, 134
positive conversations, 35
positive energy, 123, 128, 150
positive people, 34–35
Possible Human, The, 58
Powell, Mike, 50
"Power Goal Manuscript," 90
"power goaling" workshop, 39
Power of Positive Thinking, The, 124
priorities
    of college students/graduates, 75–78
    commitment to, 65, 70, 77
    determining, 71–78, 187
    focus on, 115–16, 120–21, 156–57, 179
    importance of, 63–68, 78, 83, 186
    rethinking, 164–66
    setting, 70, 73–75, 192
prioritization techniques, 66, 67
problem-solving skills, 111–12, 123–24, 193
"Pronounce All Things Good," 132–33
Psycho-Cybernetics, 58
public speaking, 37, 172

R
Ralston Purina, 138
reading, 169
recreation, 76, 162
Rehabilitation Institute, 133, 186
relaxation techniques, 54–55, 190–91
resolving matters, 146, 149
responsibility, 144, 147
results from visualizations, 43–53, 60, 84
rewards, 33–34, 72, 94–95, 148
Richards, Wendy, 82–83
Richardson, Cheryl, 160
RightPoint, Inc., 69
risks, 109–12
Robin, Vicki, 162

Rockefeller, John D., 123
Rogers, Will, 101
Roosevelt, Eleanor, 55
Rowen, Roy, 30
Rudolph, Wilma, 34
Ruth, Babe, 110

S
St. Louis University, 133, 186
St. Thomas University, 80, 182
Schwartz, Morrie, 164
Schwarzenegger, Arnold, 51–52, 58
self-affirmation, 133
self-belief, 25–26, 29, 35, 38–39, 179, 182
self-care, 160–61
self-confidence
    demonstrating, 32–33, 36–38
    developing, 23–26, 31, 34, 39, 105, 172
    and self-image, 35–36
    and success, 33–34
    and truth, 148
self-descriptions, 31
self-esteem, 39, 190
self-image, 35–36
self-importance, 27–30
self-motivation, 148
self-recognition, 33–34
seminars, 168
senses, using, 56–57
Setback Is a Setup for a Comeback, A, 110
setbacks, 110, 181, 186–87
Seven Spiritual Laws of Success, The, 161
Sill, Sterling W., 59
Six Pillars of Self-Esteem, The, 147
smiling, 129–30
"square tongue rule," 127
Stanford University, 82, 142, 183
Stevens, Bobbie, 43, 45, 55, 84, 117–18, 127, 129, 144, 156
Straka, Marilyn, 105, 187
Strangest Secret, The, 51
stress, decreasing, 54, 117–19, 135, 151, 154
student advice, 181–87
subconscious mind

and conscious mind, 30, 57–58
and negativity, 127–28
training, 30–31, 119
and visualizations, 53
success
action plan for, 101–12
and altering thoughts, 30, 41
benefits of, 110
components of, 189–90
creating, 189–95
definitions of, 24, 70–71, 78, 177–78, 189–90
increasing, 177–80
and personal integrity, 151, 180
probability of, 110
rewarding, 33–34
and self-confidence, 33–34
strategies for, 190
visualizing, 46–52, 179
see also manifestations; visualizations
Superwoman Syndrome, 63
Swan, Marcy, 29, 185

T
Tajiri, Charleen, 98–99
Take Time for Your Life, 160
taking action, 97–112
Taylor, K. D., 26, 29, 87, 143, 181
Templeton, John, 131, 151, 163, 171, 180
temptations, 141–42, 149
"Ten Commandments of Risk Taking," 111
Think and Grow Rich, 32, 58
Thoreau, Henry David, 48, 89
thoughts
altering, 30, 41
capturing, 93
controlling, 30, 51
creating experiences through, 43
"three C's," 127–28, 179
Through the Looking Glass, 80
time management, 67–69, 75, 160–61
"to do" lists, 63, 67, 73–75, 78
Toastmasters, 37
Tonight Show, The, 49

Tracy, Brian, 95
truth, 141, 145–49
Tuesdays with Morrie, 164

U
U. C. Berkeley, 76
United States Military Academy, 78, 99, 182
University of Dayton, 76, 100, 184
University of Florida, 29, 99, 182
University of Hawaii, 98
University of Maryland, 183
University of Minnesota, 27, 28
University of North Carolina, 88
University of Texas, 24
Unlimited Futures, 43, 156
Unlimited Futures: How to Understand the Life You Have and Create the Life You Want, 84
Upward Reach, The, 59
Utah State University, 94, 99, 184
Utah Valley State College, 26, 143, 181

V
values, 72–78, 83, 144, 179, 187
valuing people, 136–37, 161
Visioneering, 41
visualizations
    descriptions of, 41–44, 52–53
    exercise for, 45–46, 52–59
    of goals, 52–57, 83, 89–90
    reinforcing, 57
    results from, 43–53, 60, 84
    statements on, 58–59
    and success, 46–52, 179
    technique for, 55, 192
    see also manifestations
vos Savant, Marilyn, 30, 119

W
Wayne State University, 35, 185
Wealthy Soul series, 24
well-being, 77, 133, 146–47, 150
West Point Military Academy, 78, 99, 182
White, Kathy Brittain, 88, 115, 145

Windham, Laurie, 24–26, 115
Winfrey, Oprah, 86
Wolf, Connie, 115, 136
Wood, Nathan, 78, 187
work ethic, 182–83
workshops, 168, 185
worry, 128–29
written goals, 84–85, 95

Y
You'll See It When You Believe It, 49
Your Erroneous Zones, 49
Your Money or Your Life, 162

Z
Ziglar, Zig, 136

About the Author

Joan Eleanor Gustafson is the founder and president of Pinnacle Pathways International (www.pinnaclepathways.com). She has coached hundreds of individuals in achieving their desired results, both in their careers and in their personal lives. A world-renowned professional speaker, Joan has inspired more than 3,500 audiences through her keynote speeches and presentations.

As a business strategist, Joan focuses on her clients' objectives. Her consulting specialties include:

- Strategic and tactical planning
- Marketing excellence
- Leadership development
- Strategic outsourcing
- Maximizing results through effective employee relations and development

Prior to founding her company, Joan was a member of the Corporate Marketing Management Committee at 3M, where she held international leadership and management positions for twenty-six years. In these positions, her responsibility included the following areas:

- e-Business
- Customer satisfaction
- Knowledge management
- Communications

- Strategic outsourcing
- Sales and marketing productivity
- Information Technology

Her international responsibility included a two-year assignment in Europe, where she lived in Paris, France and maintained offices both in Paris and in Brussels, Belgium. While in Europe, she traveled 80 percent of the time to fourteen European countries to enhance 3M's marketing and sales productivity and quality in those countries.

Joan holds a B.A. degree in Business Management and an MBA in Management. She is on the faculty of University of Phoenix, where she teaches MBA courses in international management, e-Business, and strategic management. She is a member of the National Speakers Association and is a past-president of the Phoenix chapter of Professional Coaches and Mentors Association.

Joan has spoken and consulted to businesses, professionals, and college students throughout the United States, Europe, Canada and Asia. She is the author/co-author of six books on success and leadership. She can be contacted at joan@pinnaclepathways.com.